# America's Land
# and Its Uses

MARION CLAWSON, director of the Land
Use and Management Studies Program
at Resources for the Future, Inc., since
1955, is the former director of the Bureau
of Land Management, U.S. Department
of the Interior. Among his books are
*The Federal Lands*, *Land for the Future*,
*Economics of Outdoor Recreation*, and
*Policy Directions for U.S. Agriculture*.

# America's Land and Its Uses

by MARION CLAWSON

*Published for*
RESOURCES FOR THE FUTURE, INC.
by The Johns Hopkins Press
Baltimore and London

Copyright © 1972 by The Johns Hopkins Press
All rights reserved
Manufactured in the United States of America
The Johns Hopkins Press, Baltimore, Maryland 21218
The Johns Hopkins Press Ltd., London

Library of Congress Catalog Card Number 70-167985

ISBN 0-8018-1343-3 (cloth)
ISBN 0-8018-1330-1 (paper)

# *Contents*

## LIST OF TABLES

## LIST OF FIGURES

# Preface

This book is a survey of the major facts and issues about land and land policy. It does not go into details that would be of interest primarily to the specialist, and supporting evidence and reference sources are generally omitted.

The book draws upon research that my colleagues and I have conducted at Resources for the Future over the past fifteen years, as well as upon the research of others, and upon data published by government and other agencies. An earlier, more detailed, and fully documented study, *Land for the Future*, by Marion Clawson, R. Burnell Held, and C. H. Stoddard (Johns Hopkins Press, 1960), covered more or less the same ground, and has served as a basis for the present book, which is, however, updated in many respects. Other RFF books, *Economics of Outdoor Recreation*, by Marion Clawson and Jack L. Knetsch (Johns Hopkins Press, 1966), *Soil Conservation in Perspective*, by R. Burnell Held and Marion Clawson (Johns Hopkins Press, 1965), and *Policy Directions for U.S. Agriculture—Long-Range Choices in Farming and Rural Living*, by Marion Clawson (Johns Hopkins Press, 1968), have also provided useful ideas and analyses. Two paperback books, *Land for Americans* and *Land and Water for Recreation*, published by Rand McNally and Company in 1963, both written by Marion Clawson, and both now out of print, somewhat resembled the present book in length, style, and subject matter, and have provided useful antecedents to the present volume.

The clarity and readability of this book have gained much from the editing of Nora E. Roots, and I am grateful for her assistance. I also owe thanks to Diantha Stevenson, who not only typed the manuscript but did so with skill and dedication.

In writing this book I have had in mind not only the general reader, but also the needs of advanced high school courses, basic college courses, and adult education classes for reading assignments. I hope that the book will also be of value and interest to citizens' groups, such as the League of Women Voters, and to conservation, agricultural, forestry, or other groups that are concerned with particular aspects of land use.

A special feature of this book, aside from its nontechnical approach, is its treatment of all land uses on an equal or coordinate plane. There are chapters on agriculture, forestry, recreation, and urban land uses, but no one use or class of uses is singled out for special attention. There is inevitably a "miscellaneous" residual of uses—considered in the next-to-last chapter—but even these are discussed on a par with the other and more generally known major land uses. Throughout the book, an effort has been made to present information basic to issues of public policy affecting land, and to point out the relevance of these facts to such policy issues. But no program of legislation or of public action is described, much less recommended.

May 1971                                    MARION CLAWSON

*America's Land
and Its Uses*

# CHAPTER ONE

# Land in Our Daily Lives

From time immemorial, men have travelled the seas and made use of the lakes and streams, but Man is essentially a land animal. At one time land was basic for the personal income and security of all men everywhere, and even today it is the mainstay of most of the people in most of the world. Land was and is both a means of earning current livelihood and of providing for one's family. In many times and places, land has meant social position and political power as well as economic advantage. Tribes and nations have fought wars over land throughout history. Social systems, laws, and customs have all been concerned with one or another aspect of land. Land permeates every society and economy—playing a somewhat different role in less-developed economies than in the more developed ones.

In the United States today, at one level of intellectual perception, we may seem to have moved beyond this age-old concern over land. A man today may earn a living, have ample economic security now and for his old age, have a secure and advanced social position, and have significant political power, all without owning a foot of land. Our society and economy have developed in a different direction, and these measures of personal well-being are attainable by means other than landownership.

But this apparent freedom from dependence on land, or this apparent indifference to land, is deceptive. All economic and social activity in the United States has a place dimension; it all requires some land. True, a person need not own land; he may rent it, or rent structures based on it, or obtain the use of land under other arrangements. But the population as a whole is still closely dependent on land for food, fiber, shelter, and the amenities; the ultimate source of food is not the supermarket, but the land. The competition for use of land in the United States is strong and rising; land policies are still important.

The total land area of the United States is fixed (with minor exceptions, such as filling of swamps or bays) while the total population has grown and is growing. With the numerator of the land/man ratio fixed while the denominator increases, the laws of mathematics result in a smaller and smaller land area per person. Does this somehow mean that we are "running out" of land or that the supply of land is getting dangerously low?

Our concern, as individuals and as citizens, is not really with the acreage of land, but with the products and services of land. These depend not only on the area and the characteristics of the land, but also upon the inputs of labor, capital, management, and technology into various productive processes. The volume, variety, and scope of these inputs has risen greatly over the years, and promises to rise more in the decades ahead. As a result, the products and services of land are not in danger of running out, and the total land situation of the United States is relatively comfortable.

Nevertheless, there are problems in land use—problems about which every alert citizen should be informed, since as a voter and as a participant in society he will have to take positions and actions about land. In particular, the supply of desirable land in choice locations is no longer plentiful, and there are serious problems of land degradation and misuse to be corrected.

The comfortable position on land in the United States today may not extend forever; if population continues to rise at an unchecked rate, the day will come when sheer space per person will be a stringently limiting factor. But that day lies a relatively long way in the future. As a nation we may, for various reasons, wish to limit our population in the interests of the quality of life for those who do live here, but it will be some time before sheer land area becomes the controlling factor.

LAND SUPPLY PER PERSON

In 1970 the average person in the United States had the products and the use of about 11 acres of land. Some of this land is desert in the West, some is tundra in Alaska, and some is nearly barren mountain tops; but some is fertile cropland in the Corn Belt and elsewhere, some has magnificent forests, and some is the highly valuable land of our towns and cities. This is the land on which we live, work, and play, and from which we get our food and forest products. Some of it is in highways, airports, and other necessary uses for modern living. This land is owned by individuals, by groups, and by governments; and it is used by various persons and groups, but all of us benefit, in one way or another, from its existence and from its productivity.

Many persons may be uncertain about how much land 11 acres is, and a few comparisons may be helpful. It is about three average-size city blocks; it is 22 or more generous size suburban home lots. (An acre contains 43,560 square feet; the playing area of a football field is 300 by 160 feet, or 48,000 square feet, or 1.1 acres.)

By world standards, the people of the United States are extremely fortunate in their land heritage. Our total land surface per person is almost exactly the same as the world average. But our land is on the average vastly more productive than that for the world as a whole. Not more than 10 to 15 percent can reasonably be classed as wasteland; even the deserts, tundra, and mountain tops often have some value for wildlife, mineral production, watershed, or other purposes. Among the other large countries of the world, Russia and Canada have a higher percentage of their land in Arctic or near-Arctic lands with only the most limited productive capabilities; Brazil has a vast Amazon jungle which is just beginning to be exploited; Australia has a vast "dead heart" of desert or near-desert; and China has large areas of desert or near-desert.

As can be seen in figure 1, the acreage of cropland presently used for crops and rotation pasture exceeds 2 acres per capita in the United States, and there is enough potential cropland for a total of about 4 acres per capita if the need were acute. Few other urbanized and industrialized nations have anything like such a generous endowment of good cropland per person, and in many of the densely populated countries of Asia and the Middle East the figure is well below an acre per person. A large part of our favorable position is due to our relative youth as a nation. The early settlers found a highly favorable environment on the North American continent, and their technology and skills enabled them to exploit it.

OVERALL LAND USE SITUATION IN THE UNITED STATES

The "big three" of land use, on an area basis, are cropland, pasture and grazing land, and forest and woodland; but the "important two" in terms of value of land and relationship to the daily lives of many people, are urban and recreation (figure 1).

Land use statistics and relationships depend in part upon

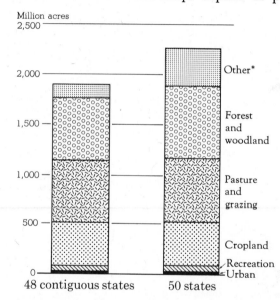

*Includes transportation, military, water management and other uses; also includes marshes, bare rock areas, sand dunes, deserts, etc.; also includes all unaccounted for areas, including idle.

Figure 1. The "big three" of land use on an area basis are grazing, forestry, and agriculture. Urban and recreation uses account for only small percentages of the land area but are the "important two" in terms of the value of the land and the number of people involved. The "other" category includes a great variety of land types and uses as well as idle land; the area in this category is substantially larger for the 50 states than for the 48 states, because so much land in Alaska is in miscellaneous uses.

whether Alaska, with its huge area (more than twice as big as Texas), is included or is omitted. Land uses are quite different in Alaska than in the conterminous 48 states, in part because of the greatly different climate of Alaska. Even uses bearing the same name are really quite different; the Alaskan forests, for example, are mostly slower growing trees, less suitable for commercial use. Moreover, land area in Alaska does not enter into the pool of uses and demands of the 48 conterminous states in the same way that land in any of the latter does. For this reason, it is often desirable to show the situation for the 48 conterminous states and for the 50 states separately, as is done in figure 1. Hawaii is so small in total area (smaller than New Jersey) that its inclusion in either group does not affect the statistical totals very much.

The data used in figure 1 are the best available but still deficient in many respects. There has never been a land use inventory in the United States that included every tract of land classified according to a uniform system. Data on land area used for various purposes come from censuses of agriculture, censuses of cities and local governments, records of federal land managing agencies, and various other sources. In spite of efforts to use comparable definitions, there is reason to suspect that omissions and overlaps occur and that the reported figures for each category are not always accurate. The "unaccounted for" segment of the "other" uses category shown in figure 1 is a wastebasket of errors. Some of this "unaccounted for" land is idle by any reasonable test. But there is idle land in other categories as well. Some cropland is idle, largely because its idleness has been paid for and encouraged as part of a federal program to reduce cropped area and thus reduce agricultural output to market demand; some grazing and forest land is also largely idle, producing little and being used little or not at all; but by far the most important idle land is acreage near cities, and sometimes within their borders, held speculatively for increases in price.

A chart showing land use at 10-year intervals, generally similar to figure 1 and at the same scale, would show relatively constant land use in the United States since 1920. When the data for 1969 are published in 1972 or 1973, they will show essentially the same picture, slightly modified by a trend toward somewhat more urban and recreation land and somewhat less cropland. Moreover, the best estimates of land use for the decades ahead suggest a closely similar picture until 2000 or later. This is simply another way of saying that the great land use changes of the nineteenth century (discussed in chapter 2) had largely run their course by about 1920. Since then, the overall statistics have shown only modest changes. However, this picture of modest change is misleading in many respects. Some overall changes have occurred: land used for cropland purposes has declined in the past decade, recreation and urban areas have increased greatly in percentage terms but are still small compared with the total land area of the nation, and other net changes have taken place. In cases where changes on some land, in some places, have been offset by opposite or different changes on other land in other locations, the "net" figure, however, tells only a small part of the story.

A corollary of the relative constancy in land use is that when changes do come, they often come hard. In the days of the frontier, a piece of land could be transformed from forest or open prairie into cropland without disturbing anyone very much; today, when a superhighway is built through an urban area, thousands of people may be disturbed, and some may lose their homes; controversy is inevitable, however beneficial the change may be overall. Land use changes in the future will generally be still more difficult—upsetting to many people, hence resisted, while at the same time beneficial to others and supported by them. A country, no less than a person, encounters new problems as it sheds the old ones.

Size and Diversity

Visitors from other lands are often amazed to find that the United States is so big and that its land types are so varied. Many Americans might experience the same feeling if they were to drive across the country instead of flying across it so high and so fast that they scarcely realize what lies beneath. Anyone who walks along our seashores, or on our farms, or visits ranches, or hikes through some of our better forests, or backpacks or canoes into the back country will soon begin to get a better idea of the vast distances.

But diversity of physical land type is as striking as distance and area. In topography and relief, our country varies from mountain ranges, especially in the East and West, to great rolling plains, to swamps and river valleys. In climate, it varies from deserts to very high rainfall in some areas, cold winters and permanent underground ice in northern Alaska, and scores of variants between. Death Valley lies below sea level, hot and nearly desolate, while less than 100 airline miles away Mount Whitney stands cold and bare as the highest point in the 48 conterminous states. As a result of climate and topography, soils development has been quite different in different regions, varying from no true soils in much of the desert and low-rainfall areas to deep well-developed soils with rich organic matter in some of the prairies and erstwhile forests. Reflecting all of these factors and more, the native vegetation ranged from magnificent forests of many types, to tall and short grass prairies, to desert shrubs.

One could go on and on, reciting true and dramatic facts about our land. Even one who has travelled widely for many years, and reads a great deal, is from time to time amazed at some natural feature of some part of the United States. It is utterly impossible, in this book, to attempt to describe even the major parts of the United States in adequate detail. One can only try to arouse the interest of the reader, to find out for himself, by direct personal experience or by reading the experiences of others, more about the land.

This matter of size and diversity of the United States has been introduced here for a different reason. With such diversity in physical land type and in use, it is dangerous to generalize without warning the reader that large and significant exceptions exist. In a book of this length and type, it is necessary to consider land use on a broad basis. It is entirely valid to use national statistics or talk about national totals and national averages, but generalizations must be appreciated for what they are. The statement that there has been little change in land

use in the United States does not mean that there has been
little change in every county in every state. For every general-
ization, there are exceptions, and sometimes exact opposites.

## Man Has Left His Mark

The early European settlers and those who came after them
have left their mark on present-day America. Extensive areas of
forests were cleared, sometimes by burning magnificent trees
merely to get rid of them; forest lands and prairies were plowed,
and left vulnerable to erosion. The grazing of domestic livestock
on native forage grasses and other plants often had serious effects
upon the plant cover; and some species of wild animals have
nearly disappeared.

Man has built reservoirs to store water for his needs, and in
so doing has brought about major ecological changes in the
reservoir areas. Through irrigation, he has transformed some
deserts and dry areas into farmland and others into salty areas
or swamps. He has built great cities, and he has polluted the
air around them. And the wastes from the cities and from industry and agriculture have led to the pollution of many rivers,
streams, and lakes. All in all, modern Man has drastically altered
the natural scene that his colonial ancestors found in the United
States; he has also developed an economy and a society of high
economic output and of luxurious personal consumption.

The Indians whom the Europeans found on this continent—
and who were themselves immigrants whose forebears came
from northern Asia many thousands of years earlier—lived more
nearly with the land, conforming their actions and lives to it,
rather than trying to change it as the Europeans did. Lest one
credit the Indians with more respect for Nature, it should be
realized that they lacked many of the tools for massive modifica-
tion of the natural scene. Until the Spaniards introduced horses,
cattle, and sheep, the Indians lacked animal power and domestic
grazing livestock; they never had the wheel or the plow, to say
nothing of the bulldozer. They did have fire, and they used it
as a conscious tool of resource management. Extensive prairies
are believed to owe their existence to repeated burning because

grasses were resistant to fire and trees were not. In other situations, forest productivity was sometimes improved by fire.

The European colonists had the technical, physical, and economic power to produce change in the natural landscape they found, and they used their power. The colonial ax may seem a feeble tool compared with the modern bulldozer as a means of clearing a forest, but in combination with fire it was the means whereby millions of acres of forest were cleared. Wooden plows pulled by oxen may likewise seem a feeble tool for land cultivation compared with modern tractors and plows, yet a lot of land was first plowed by such tools. In scores of ways, modern Man has further modified the natural environment—raped or ravaged it, some would say. But he has made some land more fertile than it was when he first found it.

It is also true that modern Man has devised institutions and mechanisms for managing and preserving land that his colonial ancestor lacked. The rise of soil conservation as a social and resource movement, the development of the national forest concept, and the establishment of national parks—the latter now imitated in many countries throughout the world—were all manifestations of the desire to find ways of managing the natural resources to meet the demands and challenges of the present and of the future.

This brief overview of resource history in the United States shows that we do not start with a clean slate today. Our task is somehow to reconcile the demands of a large and growing population with the health and condition of its natural resources. We cannot retreat to the natural environment that our colonial ancestors found, even if we wished to do so. For better or worse, we have replaced nearly all the buffalo with cattle, and our future management problem for the Great Plains lies with the cattle. We cannot avoid stream pollution by keeping everyone out of every watershed, for all land is watershed and there is no place else to live and work. The resource management problem of the future is by no means hopeless in my judgment, but its solution lies in going forward, not in trying to retreat to a bucolic past that was probably a less happy situation than is sometimes idealized.

## Land Use Is a Public Matter

Land use in the United States is controlled or influenced by public action to a greater degree than most people realize.

About a third of our total land area is publicly owned. How this came about, and how it has changed over the years, is explored in somewhat more detail in chapter 2. Most of this publicly owned land is owned by the federal government, and some by states, counties, cities, and special districts. There are good reasons to expect that the area of publicly owned land in the United States will increase, not decrease, over the decades ahead, although the changes may be small on a percentage basis. Comparatively little of the land now publicly owned will be disposed of to private owners; as a nation, we have concluded that some types of land are more likely to be used wisely if publicly owned than if privately owned. Some land now privately owned is almost certain to come into public ownership to be used for highway rights-of-way, parks, and reservoirs. If the nation gets into massive slum clearance and urban renewal, there could be a sizable increase in the area of publicly owned land in the hearts of our larger cities.

Most of the land in the United States is, and will remain, privately owned. However, government at all levels—federal, state, and local—has extensive powers over the use of private land.

First, government can exercise its power of eminent domain to take private land needed for public purposes. Prime examples of the use of this power arise with respect to highways, slum clearance, and park additions. The government's power is nearly unlimited, subject to the requirement that the land is needed for a public purpose. The courts have argued about "public purpose" many times in the past; and some land uses—slum clearance, for example—are today acceptable when once they would not have been. The private land so taken must be paid for, of course; and the private landowner can always insist upon a court-determined price for his land, which in practice has often meant a relatively generous price. What makes the power of eminent domain so important is not the area of land taken, which has been rather small and presumably will continue to be small, but the strategic nature of the lands and the coercive nature of this power.

A second basic governmental power over land is taxation. In our American system of government, taxes on land are not levied by the federal government and are not levied by many states, but real estate taxes are often the mainstay of local government. Every property owner pays taxes directly; every tenant helps to pay his landlord's taxes. Thus taxes on land and its improvements affect almost everyone. Taxes are also one of the largest costs of land ownership; they not infrequently take a fourth, a third, or even a half of the income from the land. It is not only their amount but also the way in which they are calculated and collected that may affect the landowner. In suburban and urban areas, desired governmental services, such as schools, libraries, and parks, can often be obtained only by use of real estate taxes. The homeowner is often caught between his desire for better governmental services of some kind and his dislike of paying more property taxes.

A third basic governmental power over land and landowners is the police power. The most common use of this power is in zoning ordinances. These tell the landowner what he may not do with his land, and thus by inference tell him what he may do with it. A prime purpose of zoning ordinances is to protect landowners and users from nuisances or other undesirable uses on the land in the locality. Zoning may prohibit industrial or commercial activity within a prime residential neighborhood, for instance. The value of any tract of land is in large degree determined by the uses made of surrounding or nearby areas. Zoning has most often been applied to present or potential urban and suburban areas, but it has also been applied to some rural areas. Subdivision regulations are another use of police power. By establishing minimum-size building lots, the unit of local government largely controls land use. Police power is also used as the basis for building and health codes aimed at protecting people from substandard residential structures.

The fourth, and by far the most important, basic governmental power with respect to land is the power of the public purse. Both land use and landowners are materially affected by the way in which governments at all levels, but especially the federal government, spend funds for various public purposes. The variety of such programs is so great and their scope so large that they are perhaps the most influential single force affecting land use in the United States today.

Government finances a great deal of research, which is available to landowners and others free, and which often greatly affects the decisions they make about use of their land. Government carries on some resource-managing activities directly—flood protection, irrigation, and others, which enable private landowners to carry out activities that would otherwise be difficult or impossible. The federal government has heavily subsidized highway construction, airport construction, and, especially in an earlier day, railroad construction. It has also subsidized electric power production and transmission, the latter especially into rural areas. It has provided financial help for forest fire control and for some other forest programs. And it has provided direct payments to millions of farmers to carry out soil conservation measures, to reduce crop acreage, or to carry out other programs. As a result of some of the farm programs, millions of acres of cropland have been taken out of active use and are largely idle today.

## CHANGING SPACE AND LAND USE RELATIONS

The enormous scientific, technological, social, economic, and political changes of the past two generations have greatly altered the space relationships among land tracts or areas, and the land demand-supply situations have accordingly been modified greatly. The one constant about land is its position with reference to the North Pole, the equator, and other land and water masses. Other physical features of the land may change—its forests may be cut, its soils may erode, or its surface may be paved with impervious asphalt or concrete.

Over the centuries, a major revolution in communication and in transport has both shrunk and expanded the world—shrunk it, in terms of permitting travel and freight shipments over long distances, and expanded it in the sense of opening up new areas for the use of people resident in any particular location. This situation can be illustrated with a simple example. By World War I the time distance across the United States had shrunk from a pre-railroad distance represented by the top of a moderately large dining room table to the distance shown in figure 2. Air travel cut this time distance sharply, and jet planes reduced it further. These comparisons apply to cross-country travel only; time distance reductions have been less marked for intermediate points. Pumpkin Center and Podunkville may be relatively more isolated than they ever were, as plane travel has passed them by and railway service has been reduced.

The results of this shrinking of economic space have been considerable for nearly all kinds of land uses. Distances, and

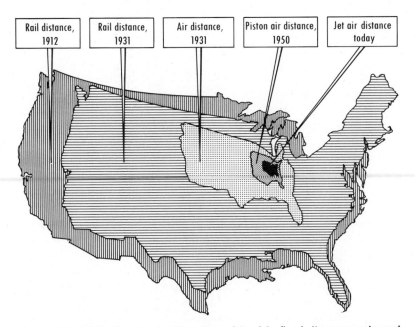

| Rail distance, 1912 | Rail distance, 1931 | Air distance, 1931 | Piston air distance, 1950 | Jet air distance today |

Figure 2.   While the physical location of land is fixed, its economic and social location changes over time. One example of this is the contraction of the nation since 1912 due to the increased speed of transportation.

costs based upon distance, are still important factors affecting land use. But, to a substantial degree, we now have national and regional markets for land and its products, whereas formerly we had local ones. Most agricultural products and many or most forest products move in a national market now. People seek outdoor recreation hundreds of miles from their home. With nearly universal automobile ownership, even the corner grocery store is exposed to competition on a wider basis. This reduction in travel times and costs has greatly increased the effective supply of land; it has also greatly increased the demand for land in the more remote locations. There are few sheltered areas today; in a remote wilderness area, one can see planes and satellites go overhead. Land problems of all kinds must increasingly be studied from a national viewpoint; the environment of each area is determined in part by conditions in other areas.

## Quality of the Environment and Land Use

In the past decade or so, there has been a dramatically rising tide of popular concern over the quality of our environment on this earth. Man has developed a highly productive economy, which supports several billion people, some in luxury. By and large, little attention has been given to the impact of this production process upon the natural environment. The goal of the production process has been to provide goods and services for the consumer; the production man has sought to make something that would appeal to consumers, the marketing man has sought to coax or beguile people into buying, and the economist has measured output in terms of what reached the consumer. Very little attention has been paid to the uses the consumer actually made of the product or service; there have been constant complaints about the quality and cost of service for autos and household gadgets. But still less attention has been paid to the wastes or the residuals from the consumption process.

This concentration on production for the consumer was misguided and incomplete. Everything that reaches the consumer shows up again in some form as a residual—waste, in more popular but less accurate terminology. The tonnages of inputs, whether measured to the individual or to a city or other large area, must be matched by the tonnages of the output. The latter may be gaseous, liquid, or solid, and many residuals may be shifted from one form to another, as when household paper wastes are burned to create added air pollution. The residuals from some processes may be valuable inputs to others.

This matter of quality of environment goes far beyond land use, and cannot be explored fully in a book about land use without distorting its length. It seems highly probable that people will demand new approaches to environmental problems, although it is as yet far from clear that all the protesters are willing to pay the costs, which may be considerable. In this larger picture, land use cannot remain unaffected. Some land will be used for landfill or for garbage dumps. But agricultural or suburban development practices that dump a lot of sediment into streams may well be curbed; and the poultry producer or beef cattle feeder, whose operations contribute to the mineral load of waters and thus to the growth of algae there, may also feel some restrictive hand. In scores of ways, an effective demand for a cleaner and more attractive natural environment may affect land use.

# CHAPTER TWO

# A Capsule History of Land in the United States

In 1492, when Columbus was sailing the ocean blue, the land that is now the United States of America was the home of about a million Indians. Some of them were primarily food gatherers, living on seeds, plant roots, berries, and the like, with a few succulent insects at times; some practiced a good bit of agriculture; some did a lot of fishing; and all of them were hunters. The Indians had fire, bows and arrows, and other tools, but they had not developed the wheel; they had dogs, but not the domesticated animals we know today. Horses, cattle, sheep, goats, and pigs were introduced much later by the Spaniards. Given their technology, the Indians had probably reached numbers that represented the carrying capacity of the land. All of the area of the present United States that was habitable at all was occupied by some tribe or tribes; there were no empty lands.

The Indians' concepts of landownership, tenure, and use were completely different from those that the European colonists brought with them. Individual landownership was apparently unknown among Indians, or at least greatly restricted; large areas were more or less the territory of tribes or groups of tribes, although boundaries were often vague and raids and wars were common. Such tribal territory represented the homeland to the groups concerned, the source of their food, the area within which they ranged seasonally or irregularly, and to which they had strong attachments. The idea of selling land, in the sense that we know it today, or in the sense that the early colonists knew it, was totally foreign to the Indians.

Out of this difference in concepts toward land was to come much misunderstanding, bitterness, and conflict in later decades.

A group of colonists or a unit of government would conclude a treaty with Indians—sometimes after a military defeat, sometimes with the aid of whiskey; the Indians were given gifts or money, and land was received in return. The Indian, at least at first, had no idea that he was surrendering all claim to the land involved, while the white man thought he had bought it in total title. Neither side was very good about keeping its bargains; the white men repeatedly trespassed beyond the land supposedly bought, pushing the Indians westward or onto reservations; if the reservations turned out to contain valuable land, the process was repeated. The Indians, for their part, liked the white man's beef at least as well as buffalo meat, and attacks on frontier settlers were common. It was an irreconcilable conflict of cultures; once the white men had established permanent settlements, the Indian culture was doomed.

Total numbers of Indians declined over the decades from about a million to a low of perhaps no more than half a million around the turn of the century. Many Indians today are not full bloods; but those considered Indian again number about a million. A few are prosperous, and some have adopted modern ways of living. But a great many live on reservations, or in small settlements mostly in the West, often in great poverty, discriminated against in many ways, unable to make personal adjustments to modern life styles and yet cut off from their own older living patterns. Among the minority racial and ethnic groups in the United States, the Indian is in by far the worst material condition, the most discriminated against, the most neglected—and this in spite of great achievements by many Indians.

## Colonial Land History

As a result of the early explorations of North America by sea expeditions from various European nations, there ensued a race among such nations to claim large chunks of the new continent for their own. At one time or another, Britain, France, Spain, Holland, Sweden, Russia, and other countries asserted claims to territory that is now within the United States. Their rivalries led to armed clashes in the territories, and sometimes to threats of war at home. The Pope was asked by Spain to arbitrate claims. Everyone ignored the fact that all the land involved was the home of Indians, although the latter were sometimes placated by treaties and gifts.

In the seventeenth and eighteenth centuries, Britain came to be the dominant colonial power in what is now the eastern United States, though Spain held Florida. Today, we often overlook the fact that our colonial history was nearly as long as our national history. If the colonial period is defined as beginning with Jamestown in 1607 and ending with the Declaration of Independence in 1776, it embraces 169 years; the national period covers less than 200 years if dated from 1776, and still less if dated from the year when independence was actually won. More important than the length of the colonial period, however, are the attitudes toward land—and the policies about land—that developed during those years. The national land history is in many respects but the natural flowering of colonial land history.

First of all, the concepts of landownership were firmly established in colonial times. They evolved nearly everywhere into the concept of fee simple ownership; the land was the absolute property of its owner to do with as he wished without interference from any others, including government. He was regarded as owning the land "from the center of the earth to the zenith of the sky"; the idea that the King owned the minerals, common in Europe, especially in lands whose legal codes derived from Roman origins, was replaced by the idea that the owner of the surface also owned the minerals—with results that have carried over to today. As part of this concept of fee simple ownership, the owner came to have absolute power over its bequeathal to heirs; primogeniture, entails, and other restrictions on inheritance were gradually abolished. During the nineteenth century, fee simple ownership was the basis upon which the farmer used his land as he saw fit, regardless of erosion or damage to others, and upon which the city landowner also did as he chose upon his land; it was not until later that restrictions on land use were superimposed on fee simple ownership.

The idea of widespread landownership took hold and became

a fact during the colonial period. In a country where land was abundant, but workers and capital scarce, it was probably inevitable that landownership should be widely spread. Some colonizers undertook to settle colonists on long-term leases, with annual quitrents, but this system led to bitter controversy, and in the end the landlords lost their quitrents. True, there were exceptions to the idea of widespread ownership of land; in the early days, plantations were common in the southern colonies and not unknown elsewhere; and later, large landholdings were built up in the Midwest and Far West by various land speculators and owners. But, throughout, the family holding was dominant economically and often politically and socially as well.

The colonial land history had other aspects that have persisted to the present. Land gradually came to be a commodity, and fortunes were made through land transactions. Most of the prominent citizens in the colonial period—and many in the national period—were active speculators in land. The suburban land speculator of today is their descendant. Many settlers had a deep emotional attachment to land; this was especially true of first-generation immigrants who could never have owned land at home and who came in part because of the opportunity to acquire land. But even these people, or their children, were not always averse to taking advantage of rising land prices.

The abundance of land and the shortage of labor during the colonial period led to many devices to import workers, some of which have left deep scars. Workers were brought from England on an indenture system; the man worked a term of years (usually seven) to repay the cost of his passage, after which he was free to follow his own pursuits; sometimes he was given a tract of unimproved land. American colonies were sometimes used as an outlet for deprived social classes in Britain—Georgia was first settled by prisoners and ex-prisoners. But the arrangement with the most serious and most lasting effects was Negro slavery. Negroes were captured, or more frequently bought from Negro chieftains who had captured them, especially along the West African coast where modern Nigeria and other new nations are located. Their ways of life were very different; a large proportion of them died on the long sea voyages, undertaken under

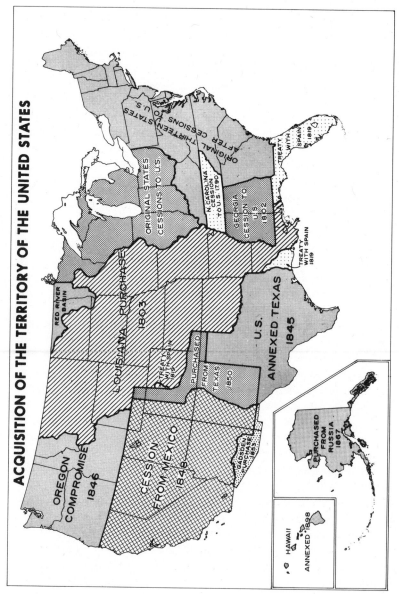

# ACQUISITION OF THE TERRITORY OF THE UNITED STATES

Figure 3.

very bad conditions at a time when any sea voyage was hardship by modern standards; and they were forced to work under conditions where most colonists were unwilling to work themselves. The origins of the racial problem in the United States today go back to the colonial land use situations.

The immigrants from Europe also faced great hardships, and death rates among early colonists were high—as indeed they were in their home lands. But immigrants have always experienced difficulties, and been forced to accept poor and dangerous employments. I recall reading the account of a Mississippi planter in the antebellum days, who was clearing some delta land to grow cotton; he chose to hire Irish immigrants, not caring to risk his valuable slaves in the malaria-infested swamps and jungles.

## U.S. Territorial Expansion

During the first half of the nineteenth century, the United States expanded its territory immensely (figure 3). The original thirteen states, when they won their independence, owned the United States as far west as the Mississippi River, except for Florida and a small area around New Orleans. Some of the old colonies, now states, had large territorial claims—Connecticut and Virginia, for instance; others, as New Jersey, had no claims to land outside their boundaries. As part of the political bargains that led to the Union, the states with land claims relinquished them (sometimes with strings attached) to the new national government between 1781 and 1802. The Northwest Ordinance of 1785 provided, among other matters, that the territory north of the Ohio River should be divided into states which would be on an equal footing with the original states in every respect.

The first great acquisition of territory was the purchase of Louisiana from France for $15 million in 1803. This land, representing nearly a fourth of the area of the conterminous 48 states, has since become all or part of thirteen states. The purchase proved to be a great bargain, in large part because it got one major European power out of our present territory, and in part because it secured control over the Mississippi River, as well as over such a large area of land. Florida was purchased from Spain in 1819. Texas won its independence from Mexico in 1836 and, after a few years as an independent republic, was annexed to the United States in 1845. After a war with Mexico in 1848, the United States annexed the Pacific Southwest, including California, and later bought from Mexico a large piece of southern Arizona (the Gadsden Purchase). A treaty with Great Britain in 1846 resolved the boundary dispute in the Pacific Northwest. In 1867 Alaska was bought from Russia. Other acquisitions included the annexation of Hawaii, previously an independent kingdom, in 1898. These territorial acquisitions were a major achievement for what had begun as a small, thinly populated, and poor new nation.

The land in the territories so acquired, with the exception of the relatively small areas in private ownership at the time of acquisition, became the property of the U.S. government in a proprietary as well as in a governmental sense. Deciding what lands were already privately owned was a difficult matter because land records were typically defective in the territories. There was undoubtedly a great deal of fraud by some claimants who were dealt with overgenerously, but many small owners may have been defrauded of their rights. In recent years, groups in New Mexico and elsewhere have tried to claim land they assert properly belongs to them by inheritance from their ancestors whose claims were not recognized.

The acquisition of these territories began a history of federal lands which has continued to the present (figure 4). The disposal and management periods of this history are considered briefly in the sections that follow.

FEDERAL LAND DISPOSAL

The dominant political philosophy at the time of independence and for 100 years thereafter was that the newly acquired land, like the land in the original colonies, would be disposed of to settlers. There were many political struggles over the terms and the forms of that disposal, but none, for a long time,

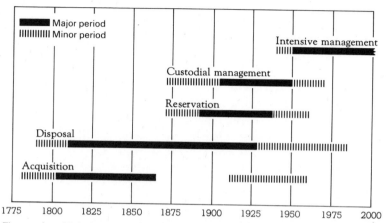

Figure 4. Major eras in federal landownership and land management in the United States, 1781–2000. As the federal lands have become more valuable and in greater demand, their management has become more intensive.

over the desirability of ultimate disposal to private owners. One group, often identified with Alexander Hamilton, wanted to sell the lands to raise money, primarily to restore to par the value of the greatly depreciated currency of the new country; another group, identified with Thomas Jefferson, wanted to make the new lands the basis for settlement of landowning farmers and regarded revenue as a secondary consideration. The laws would suggest that Hamilton won, since provision was made for sale of land on terms that favored large speculative buyers; however, the area of land sold and the money received were alike very small for the first 25 years or more of nationhood. There was simply too much land, located nearer settlements, in the hands of the states and of individuals for anyone to pay very much for land on the frontier.

In time, the terms of the laws governing the disposal of the federal lands, and the methods of land sale, came to favor easier and easier acquisition. The Homestead Act of 1862 gave a settler up to 160 acres of land in return for his residence on it for five years, some improvements, and payment of very modest fees. Other acts were equally or more generous. Sizable amounts of land were granted to states for public purposes such as schools; large areas of swampy or overflowed land were also granted to the states in the hope that they would reclaim them—half of Florida was conveyed to the state in this way. Other large grants were made to stimulate railroad construction, and some were made for canals and highways.

The federal government surveyed the lands before disposal, and its rectangular survey system has left its mark across much of the nation—a mark that is likely to persist for many generations. The government established systems of land records, which, despite some deficiencies and errors, have proven generally dependable. Today, land titles in the United States are relatively secure and safe, and usually go back to the original disposition from the federal government.

The process of land disposal dominated early American history and was a major political and social force throughout the nineteenth century. It was headlong, even heedless, and two-thirds of all the land in the 48 conterminous states moved out of the public domain, mostly into private ownership. Many of the laws were too badly designed to accomplish what the sponsors said they wanted; many laws were inconsistent with others, overlapping and somewhat nullifying but not repealing laws already on the books; and laws were administered poorly, in large part because of inadequate funds. And frauds in land disposal were rampant, as was speculation in public land or land in the process of land transfer. Settlers on the frontier, by illegal or extralegal methods, often succeeded in getting the laws applied in ways not intended by the Congress.

Whatever its limitations, the disposal of federal lands was a vital part of the process that transformed a small nation along the Atlantic Coast into a large and powerful nation occupying the whole of the central North American continent. It may well be doubted that the individuals whose spirits and energy led them to colonize and develop the frontier could have been controlled into a more orderly process. No one was in a mood to move slowly and learn from experience. People were anxious to get a piece of land while the getting was good, and on the best terms possible; the nation as a whole was obsessed with growth and expansion, and not inclined to be fussy about a few frauds or a little resource wastage as long as growth continued unabated. Moreover, this rapid settlement of the midcontinent clearly removed any threat of other nations attempting to acquire or settle it. Today most people are unaware that Russia occupied Fort Ross, about 100 miles north of San Francisco, as late as 1841.

## PUBLIC LAND RESERVATION AND MANAGEMENT

During the headlong westward push, much timber was cut from federal land in trespass, and private forests were cut, the land gutted, and abandoned. These practices continued for some time before thoughtful citizens became disturbed about what was happening and began to make demands for permanent reservation of some lands in federal ownership. A small amount of land had been reserved earlier for public purposes such as lighthouses or coast guard stations, but people now wanted much more than this. The first really large federal land reservation was Yellowstone National Park, for which 1.9 million acres were set aside in 1872; but it was not until the Forest Reserve Act was passed in 1891 that the first *system* of federal land reservation was established. Various other forms of permanent federal land reservation followed. Reservation history is as complicated as disposal history, and cannot be traced here in any detail. In addition to the reservation of land already in federal ownership, land was purchased from private individuals or states. The latter practice began after the passage of the Weeks Act in 1911, which authorized purchasing land to add to the national forests in areas where there were no federal lands remaining.

The federally owned lands were the subject of a study by the Public Land Law Review Commission, a special commission created by Congress in 1964. In its report, *One Third of the Nation's Land* (1970), the Commission proposed a number of changes in federal land administration, some of which will require Congressional action; these are likely to be the center of discussion and debate for several years.

At present there are the following major kinds of federal lands:

|  | million acres |
|---|---|
| National forests, administered by the Forest Service, U.S. Department of Agriculture | 187 |
| Grazing districts and other remaining federal land, administered by the Bureau of Land Management, U.S. Department of the Interior | 470 |
| National Parks, national monuments, and other units of the national park system, administered by the National Park Service, U.S. Department of the Interior | 23 |
| Wildlife refuges, administered by the Bureau of Sport Fisheries and Wildlife, U.S. Department of the Interior | 27 |
| Reclamation withdrawals, administered by the Bureau of Reclamation, U.S. Department of the Interior | 9 |
| Military bases, bombing ranges, and other lands administered by the U.S. Department of Defense | 31 |
| All other federal holdings | 8 |
| Total | 755 |

The early management of these lands, after their reservation, was largely custodial: fighting forest and grass fires, keeping out or apprehending trespassers, making small sales of timber, regulating grazing, serving the needs of limited numbers of recreation visitors, making modest improvements, and the like. Gradually, as the demand for the resources of these lands rose, the management became more intensive. Today, more than $500 million is spent annually in administering these lands. Government agencies supervise the cutting of large volumes of timber and the grazing of millions of livestock; they manage recreation areas visited by millions of persons. At the same time, the lands under public management produce large amounts of public revenue.

Other levels of government also own land that has to be administered. Many states received substantial grants of land from the federal government, and these and other states have purchased land for particular purposes, such as parks. In addition,

cities and counties generally own recreation land, and sometimes land for other purposes. Some unit of government owns
the land included in our roads, highways, and streets, and in
most of our airports. Still other areas are owned for reservoir and
other water management purposes.

All in all, public ownership of land in the United States is
highly important. Ours is a private ownership society in many
ways, but we have not found extensive public ownership of land
incompatible with a private ownership philosophy. One reason
is that the publicly owned lands are widely used by private business and by individuals. Though publicly owned, the land is
dominantly privately used.

## Direct Federal Intervention in Land Use

In addition to its programs of managing federal land, and of
granting federal land to states and others as a stimulant to various kinds of public improvement, the federal government has
intervened directly in a number of land use situations. For well
over 100 years, it has improved navigation on rivers and in har-
bors, thereby indirectly affecting land use. For several decades, it
has erected flood protection works (levees and dams, primarily)
which have greatly influenced land use in the protected areas.
It has engaged in a rather large-scale program of irrigation development, by means of which dry or desert lands have been
brought into productive agriculture. In the past 30 or 40 years,
it has had various programs to reduce crop acreage; in recent
years, perhaps 50 million acres of cropland have been taken out
of production under these programs. A less direct but possibly
more influential program has been the research conducted by
federal agencies or financed by federal grants to universities;
these programs have brought great improvements in the ways in
which land is used and in its productivity. In the U.S. system of
government, land taxation, direct controls over land use, and
many other programs affecting land are conducted by the states
and local government. Nevertheless, the federal government does
play an important direct role in affecting the use of private land.

PUBLIC CONTROLS OVER PRIVATE LAND USE

Under the fee simple system of private ownership, which became entrenched during the national period, a person had a legal right to use his land as he chose unless someone could prove direct personal harm; in fact, there was almost no restraint on private land use, especially throughout the nineteenth century. A person could cut his forest without thought or care about growth of a new forest—and many did; or a farmer could farm without concern over soil erosion—and many did.

But the pendulum swung back from this unrestrained individual freedom in land use. The rise of permanent federal land holdings late in the nineteenth century was one reaction. But farmers and other rural landowners were willing to impose controls when the practical situation demanded it. An early form of public control was exercised by weed control districts; farmers were unwilling to sit by helplessly and wait for their land to be invaded by the noxious weeds that were multiplying on a neighbor's land. Measures were enacted to force the farmer to control serious weed pests, or have the district take over and do this at the farmer's expense. Drainage districts were organized, and farmers who benefited from the work had to pay their share of drainage costs; irrigation districts were organized, and farmers could be forced to pay for irrigation water even if they chose not to use it. Although farmers tend to be strongly individualistic, they are willing to bring compulsion to bear on their neighbors when, in their judgment, the practical facts of the situation require it.

In urban areas, the extension of public controls over private land use has been even greater. The value of a piece of urban property is peculiarly dependent upon what is done with neighboring property; to use an extreme case, an old-fashioned glue factory producing intolerable smells will certainly destroy the value of nearby property. Even a gasoline service station, a store, or an office building is unwanted in a good residential neighborhood. To prevent the introduction of nonconforming and incompatible land uses, zoning ordinances are enacted. The zoning method was given an immense stimulus by the preparation of a suggested model land-zoning ordinance, by the Department of Commerce in the 1920s, under the personal stimulus of Herbert Hoover, then its Secretary. Land zoning won a major legal victory with the Supreme Court decision of 1926 which upheld the action of the Village of Euclid (near Cleveland, Ohio) in limiting the purposes for which the land could be used. In land planning circles, "Euclidean" refers to this decision—not to a system of mathematics.

Zoning is widely used in American cities today, and in some county areas outside of cities. Its limitations are primarily political, rather than legal. In established urban areas, a proposed change in zoning is likely to draw opponents as well as supporters, and the final decision of the zoning agency reflects a balance between the contending parties while resting on the facts of the case. In developing suburban areas, there is often no effective political countervailing power, and the landowner generally—but not always—gets his way about rezoning.

Cities have also enacted subdivision ordinances, which specify the size and other characteristics of permissible lots; building codes, which specify the kinds of materials, standards of construction, and other features of buildings, in order to keep fire and other risks to a minimum; and health ordinances, which specify standards of maintenance (or neglect) for residential and other buildings. In these and in other ways the public, operating through government at some level, has restricted the use that the individual may make of his land. Compared with practices in most European countries, land use is still relatively uncontrolled; but controls are much tighter now than they were in the past, and will surely become even tighter in the future with more and more people living in relatively close proximity.

# CHAPTER THREE

# Urban Land

The United States is an urban nation and rapidly becoming more urban with each passing year. In 1970, 73 percent of its population was "urban" (the difficulties of definition of such terms is explored later) ; World War I marked the time when the urban and rural populations were about equal. At the beginning of our national history, we were dominantly rural and small village; the big city is a product of the later nineteenth century and the twentieth century.

The value of all urban land is now about 50 percent greater than the value of all rural land, in spite of the tiny fraction of the land in urban use, as shown in figure 1 of chapter 1. Well-located urban land, suitable for a variety of uses, is scarce and valuable and always will be, in spite of ample land area for urban purposes located on the fringes of the cities and metropolises. The problem of achieving maximum efficiency in urban land use is accordingly important, but this importance is not well measured merely by the area of land involved.

Cities and metropolises play a dominant role in the economic, social, and political life of the country also. If a man from Mars (or from some more hospitable planet in another solar system), were to approach the earth, he might well regard the cities as the ganglia and the highways as the nerves reaching into the rural mass of fleshy tissue. Whether one loves the cities, or hates them, or merely observes their functioning, he cannot but be impressed today with their importance in the lives of the American people.

## DEFINITIONAL PROBLEMS

Any discussion of urban land use, or of any other problem relating to cities, is plagued by the lack of precise and widely accepted terms. As is so often the case in a changing scene, we use old words to express both old and new meanings, to everyone's confusion. "City" is one of these words.

Once upon a time, a city was rather sharply and clearly set off from its surrounding countryside; indeed, many older cities had walls around them, as a defense against attackers. In peaceful times, a few people would build homes outside the walls, to escape the crowding within, but in time of war they scurried back inside. Such cities were economic entities where manufacturing, trade, and business were located as well as residences, churches, and schools. They were also legal or political entities. For some hundreds of years, many European cities were city-states, that looked after their own defense, minted their own coinage, and conducted their affairs like a self-governing state. A hundred years ago or so, American cities were also distinct physical, economic, and political entities, sharply and clearly set off from their hinterland.

All of this has changed in recent decades. Today, there is rarely a sharp clean line between the developed city and the unbuilt-upon rural countryside; instead, some suburbs or subdivisions are usually located well out into the country, sometimes several miles from one another and from the city center where many of the residents are employed. The legal or political city has often expanded its boundaries, but rarely fast enough to keep up with the spread of the physical city. Increasingly, the old legal or political city is surrounded by other smaller cities or towns, politically separate, or by unincorporated areas typically governed as part of a county. The discrepancy between the physical-economic city on the one hand, and the legal-political city on the other, is serious and growing larger.

What term most unequivocally describes the situation? Does a reference to Washington, D.C., mean the economic and physical city; the agglomeration of people centered around the old city; or the legal city, which today has only about 30 percent of the total population of the larger city? Morever, in the case of Washington, the outlying parts are in two states, about half a dozen counties, and several satellite cities. Sometimes, the context in which a person uses "Washington" or any other city name will make it clear what he means, but sometimes not. If he speaks of Washington in contrast with Baltimore or Philadelphia, it is probable that it is the physical-economic city he has in mind; but if he speaks of Washington in contrast with Prince George's County (Maryland), it is probably the legal-political city he has in mind. I shall try to make clear, in this chapter, which kind of city I have in mind, even if this sometimes requires the use of awkward phrases such as "urban agglomeration."

In an effort to provide meaningful data about this changing city, the federal data-gathering and data-publishing agencies have developed at least two concepts over the past generation. One is the Standard Metropolitan Statistical Area (SMSA), which includes a core city or twin cities with 50,000 or more people and surrounding territory closely linked economically to the core. Various specific rules are used to determine if the linkage is close enough to warrant identification with the core. However, the boundaries follow lines of counties (and, in New England, "towns") so that a good deal of territory may be included that is only remotely related economically to the core. For instance, millions of acres of the Mohave Desert in southern California are included in the San Bernardino-Riverside SMSA; and much of my favorite canoe wilderness in northern Minnesota, reaching right up to the Canadian boundary, is in the Duluth-Superior SMSA. But even in less extreme cases, the area of basically rural territory included may be considerable.

The SMSA is a good concept to measure population, employment, and similar aspects of life of a large urban agglomeration. It is relatively inclusive and thus presents a reasonably complete picture of the physical-economic situation for a given "city." However, the SMSA includes so much rural land that its value for land use studies is limited, at best, and may even be negative if unwary persons interpret SMSA data as referring to land in urban use only.

The situation is further complicated by the fact that metropolitan regional planning agencies define their metropolitan regions for their own purposes, and their definitions are not necessarily the same as those used by the federal agencies. For instance, the New York Regional Plan Association and the Delaware Valley Regional Planning Commission (Philadelphia) have each defined their respective regions more inclusively than have the federal agencies; and each has included the Trenton (New Jersey) SMSA in its planning region.

In part because the SMSAs did include so much rural territory, the Bureau of the Census established the concept of "urbanized area" for the 1950 and later censuses. Basically, the idea was to delineate the areas actually used for urban purposes, and to compile population and other data for such areas. But any such attempt is plagued by the discontinuity of settlement around the fringes of the "cities." The Bureau of the Census developed a rather elaborate set of rules for deciding whether to include or exclude a particular suburb or subdivision in the urbanized area for a larger urban agglomeration. In practice, a good deal of idle land has been included in the urbanized areas; perhaps as much as 30 percent of their areas is undeveloped but developable land. Unfortunately, the rules were modified somewhat and the way they were applied was altered a great deal between the 1950 and 1960 censuses, so that urbanized areas of the same name may in fact not be comparable at all between these two dates. The rules and their application are still different for the 1970 census, making it only dubiously comparable with either of its predecessors.

These experiences are cited to warn the reader that published statistics may not mean what he thinks they mean. The agencies concerned have done as well, perhaps, as anyone could have done. The basic difficulty is the changing situation.

SPATIAL REDISTRIBUTION OF POPULATION

The modern population agglomerations in the United States must be viewed in a historical perspective, if they are to be fully understood. The nineteenth century was dominated economically, politically, and socially by the westward movement of people. Explorers, trappers and fur traders, gold miners, cattlemen, homesteaders, merchants, and others followed one another in rapid and sometimes bewildering succession, reaching into every corner of the country. In 1890 the Bureau of the Census was no longer able to define a frontier. Forests were cut, forest and prairie were plowed for crops, roads and railroads were built, towns were established, and other settlement actions were taken in one of the largest colonization episodes in world history. About a billion acres of land passed from public to private ownership in one of the greatest transfers of property of world history. It was a spatial redistribution of population on a grand scale; it was primarily concerned with land use, landownership, and land speculation. This essentially nineteenth century phenomenon continued to some extent until World War I.

By the middle of the twentieth century, Americans were engaged in another spatial redistribution. Now, we are partially emptying out the rural countryside; in each of the decades of the 1940s, the 1950s, and the 1960s, about half of all counties lost population. Moreover, about 60 percent of these (or about a third of all counties) lost population in all three decades—and some had lost in two or more earlier decades as well. Moreover, population losses to date are misleadingly small because they have been predominantly of the younger people; as time goes on, and the older people die, the rural population losses will be greater. At the same time, the urban agglomerations as a whole— and especially the larger ones—have been growing rather rapidly. From a national viewpoint, the population redistribution is one of concentration.

But major changes have been taking place within the urban agglomerations. In particular, people have been moving to the suburbs. The available data are less than perfect, partly because city boundaries have changed and population figures relate to changing areas. But it is clear that many older cities have gained little or not at all, and that some have lost population in the past 30 years or so. The net increases have all been around the edges of the urban-developed areas of a generation ago; most of these have been outside the old legal-political city. Thus, at a metropolitan scale, the spatial redistribution is one of dispersion. As so often happens with socioeconomic situations and problems, a closer look reveals a different scene than does a casual glance.

All spatial redistributions of population have age, sex, income, racial, and other sociological aspects. The American Negro has been transformed from dominantly rural before World War II, into dominantly urban, and big city, today. Many cities now have a large black core, and many of the residents are relatively recent migrants. The suburbs are dominantly white—"lily white," in many cases. The nineteenth century westward migration was heavily dominated by young people, and much more male than female. The mid-twentieth century migrations, especially the rural-urban migrations, also tend to be composed of young people, but the sexes are about equally represented. The migration from city center to suburb has been largely a movement of young married couples with small children, although other ages and other stages in the life cycle have also been represented. The whites living in the older city cores tend to be the old or the young, the poor or the rich; there are few in the middle years or in the middle-income range.

Many writers have been much concerned with the social segregation of race, age, and income which the mid-twentieth century migrations are producing. De facto racial segregation is often replacing de jure racial segregation. It is often assumed that this process will continue, and that the day will come when every city core is either black or else very old, very young, very rich, or very poor white, and that the suburbs will continue to be middle-aged, middle-class white. This may or may not prove to be true; it is altogether possible that racial and ethnic minorities will break out of the older city and locate in some suburbs, and that the city centers will be rebuilt differently. We simply do not know what will happen. In view of the changing history, one may well expect dynamic changes in *some* direction, even if he is not sure which direction.

## Urban Land Use Situation in 1960

If we are to have meaningful data on urban land use, we must define our terms, particularly since many figures have been circulated whose meaning is unclear. The land within a homeowner's lot is rather obviously "used" by him and his family, even if some of it is used much less intensively than the rest; so is the land in the street in front of his house, the shopping center where his wife buys groceries, the office building where he works, the schoolgrounds where his children go to school, and so on. I would also include as "used" all open space within the city if it were clearly dedicated to remaining in open space. Thus, parks, plazas, sports areas, and other open areas might lack buildings and still be used actively by many people. This is the definition of land use which the city planner is likely to use.

But there is a great deal of land in and around cities which is not "used" in this sense; it is idle, yet the presence of the city and the prospect of future expansion by the city have combined to take it out of any other use. I have called this land "withdrawn" because the city withdraws it from other use. The idle portion of the withdrawn area is about as large as the area actually used for urban purposes, as nearly as I can tell. The difference between total withdrawn area (both idle and used land) and used area is roughly analogous to the difference between gross and net weight of a package and its contents. Idle land comes in units of varying size, different ownership, and different relationship to the developed areas. There are vacant lots within the rather fully developed areas; there are some larger tracts (ranging in size from a few lots to a hundred or more lots) within the older developed areas, but most of them are nearer the suburban growing edge; and there is a band of idle land around most larger cities. Farmers sell and get out, as cities expand, partly because agriculture encounters increasing difficulty and resentment near settled areas, but partly to take advantage of the price offered by a land dealer or speculator. When land is bought for speculative purposes, it is usually left idle so that it is immediately available for sale to a developer; the speculator is unlikely to try to obtain a limited income from farming or forestry because this might restrict his ability to move quickly when opportunity presented itself.

The results of any land use study of any area tend to be determined by the "grain" of the study. For instance, the Bureau of the Census classifies counties as "urban" if they have an overall density of 1,000 or more persons per square mile. However, this does not necessarily mean that all the land in an "urban" county is in use. Data for much smaller areas—ideally, lot by lot or parcel by parcel—would reveal that many urbanized counties contain a great deal of land that is, in fact, idle and available for development. Data for large areas, which in effect average the situation within an area, have advantages for many purposes; the difficulty arises when such data are applied to all land within an area, either explicitly or implicitly.

In chapter 1, in figure 1, about 19 million acres of land were shown as "urban" in 1960. This estimate was made as part of a study trying to classify all land in the United States according to its major use. The urban acreage included that in small towns with populations of over 1,000, as well as that in larger cities. It excluded "large non-built-up areas," especially in the New England "towns." (A town in New England is not an incorporated urban unit but a political and territorial unit; it is like a mini-county, and may include a great deal of rural territory.) Given these definitions, the 19 million acres reported is probably closer to a "used" than a "withdrawn" definition, although the data rather clearly included a considerable area of idle land. The larger withdrawn areas around the periphery of cities are probably largely included in other use categories in figure 1.

In 1960, 212 SMSAs were delineated and data compiled and published for them (table 1). They included almost 200 million acres of land, or about 8½ percent of the total land area; but a great deal of this was *not* urban in use by any reasonable standard; they also included 62 percent of the total population of the nation. Since 1960, their share of population has risen further. In the same census data, 678 urbanized areas were delimited; each SMSA had at least one, but most were smaller areas outside the SMSAs. The urbanized areas included only 17 million acres of land, or well under 1 percent of the total land area, and included 69 percent of all the people. The total urbanized area in table 1 is rather close to the total "urban" area in figure 1; but, if one compares particular states or smaller areas, the apparent conformity is much smaller. Studies we have made suggest that urbanized areas are at least 30 percent idle, but how much of this idle land is included in the "urban" category of figure 1 is not clear. The data for urbanized areas include many whole "towns" in New England, which, as we have noted, are often mostly rural in their land use; the larger tracts of such rural land were excluded from "urban" in figure 1. In 1960 there were 760 cities (in the legal sense) with populations of 25,000 and over; they occupied even less land, and had a smaller proportion of all the people. And there were many smaller cities with populations of over 2,500 and less than 25,000 not shown in the table. It is in these smaller cities that land is used most lavishly—large lots, sometimes gardens, few high rise buildings, and much vacant land.

Special importance attaches to the Northeastern Urban Complex, the data for which are shown also in table 1. This is by far the most heavily urbanized region of the United States, and the

TABLE 1. NUMBER, LAND AREA, AND POPULATION OF URBAN AGGLOMERATIONS BY DIFFERENT DEFINITIONS, UNITED STATES AS A WHOLE AND NORTHEASTERN URBAN COMPLEX

| Kind of urban area | Item and unit | United States as a whole | | Northeastern Urban Complex[3] |
|---|---|---|---|---|
| | | 1970[1] | 1960[2] | 1960 |
| Standard Metropolitan Statistical Areas | Number | 230 | 212 | 34 |
| | Area (million acres) | | 198.2 | 13.8 |
| | Population (millions) | 136.3 | 112.9 | 31.7 |
| Urbanized areas | Number | | 678 | 34 |
| | Area (million acres) | | 17.4 | 3.4 |
| | Population (millions) | 149.2 | 126.6 | 28.5 |
| Cities of over 25,000 population | Number | | 760 | 109 |
| | Area (million acres) | | 10.1 | 1.2 |
| | Population (millions) | | 79.6 | 19.4 |

*Source:* U. S. Bureau of the Census, *Census of Population,* 1960 and 1970.

[1] At the time this book was written (spring 1971), only preliminary data were available for the 1970 Census, hence this column cannot be completed. When 1970 data are fully available, the figures will be larger than they were in 1960.

[2] The United States in 1960 included 2,314 million acres and 180 million persons.

[3] As defined in special studies at Resources for the Future; includes Boston SMSA on the north, Washington SMSA on the south, and intervening SMSAs and rural counties. Total area in 1960 was 20.1 million acres, total population 34.2 million people.

largest in terms of its total population. It included 34 SMSAs in 1960, or about 15 percent of all those in the country; its SMSAs included about 17 percent of the country's total population of 180 million. Urban land use is more concentrated and more intensive here than elsewhere in the country; this conclusion holds whether SMSAs, urbanized areas, or cities are the basis for comparison.

Some measure of land use within the larger cities is provided by the data in table 2. Even in these larger cities, a considerable part of the land area is reported as privately owned and "undeveloped." In a city where land use is very intensive, one would

TABLE 2. PERCENT OF LAND AREA IN VARIOUS USES, TWO GROUPS OF LARGE CITIES

*(percent)*

| Type of land use | Cities of 100,000 and over | | Cities of 250,000 and over | |
|---|---|---|---|---|
| | Whole city | "Developed" part | Whole city | "Developed" part |
| Undeveloped, privately owned | 22.3 | 0 | 12.5 | 0 |
| Public streets | 17.5 | 23.6 | 18.3 | 20.9 |
| Privately owned and used | | | | |
| Residential | 31.6 | 40.7 | 32.3 | 36.9 |
| Commercial | 4.1 | 5.3 | 4.4 | 5.0 |
| Industrial | 4.7 | 6.1 | 5.4 | 6.2 |
| Railroads | 1.7 | 2.2 | 2.4 | 2.7 |
| Publicly and semi-publicly owned (excluding streets) | | | | |
| Recreational areas | 4.9 | 6.3 | 5.3 | 6.1 |
| Schools and colleges | 2.3 | 3.0 | 1.8 | 2.1 |
| Airports | 2.0 | 2.6 | 2.5 | 2.9 |
| Cemeteries | 1.0 | 1.3 | 1.1 | 1.3 |
| Public housing | 0.5 | 0.6 | 0.4 | 0.5 |
| Other (by subtraction) | 3.0 | 3.9 | 5.1 | 5.8 |
| Total[1] | 100.0 | 100.0 | 100.0 | 100.0 |

*Source:* Adapted from "Study No. 2: Land Use in 106 Large Cities," in Allen D. Manvel, *Three Land Research Studies*, prepared for The National Commission on Urban Problems, Research Report No. 12 (Washington, D. C.: Government Printing Office, 1968).

[1] Owing to the way these data had to be compiled, the figures do not add to the totals.

expect to find a small acreage undeveloped at any given moment in time—some would simply be between uses, cleared from its former use and not yet in its new use. But one would surely not expect such idle or transitional land to exceed 2 or 3 percent. The 12.5 percent reported as "undeveloped, privately owned" in table 2 suggests that a city's boundaries were drawn too inclusively to begin with—so that a lot of idle land has always been included—or that idle land was held by speculators in hopes of a price rise, or a combination of both. Available data suggest that the percentage of undeveloped land is far greater in the smaller cities than it is in these larger ones, and that it would be still larger if the basis of analysis were the physical-economic city rather than the legal-political one.

Of the used land, residential use clearly dominates, with streets in a strong second position. If streets (most of which are in residential areas) are combined with the actual residential use, then half or more of the total used area in these larger cities is residential. Each of the other land uses is much smaller in area. If there were comparable data on land values, it is probable that the value of land in other private uses would exceed the value of land in residential use, perhaps by a wide margin, because land value per acre is much higher for the commercial and industrial uses than for residential use. Likewise, if one could devise a satisfactory index of "importance," the commercial and industrial uses would rank very much higher than their acreage alone suggests.

Some hint of the mixture of idle and used land is provided in figure 5, which is taken from a map prepared by the New York Regional Plan Association; the data came from aerial photographs and hence permitted a rather detailed delineation of the used areas. At this scale, the smallest used areas shown on the map are perhaps 40 acres in size—modest suburban subdivisions. The area is part of the New York SMSA and within the economic hinterland of New York City; the land use situation shown is at the end of 1964. Some of this area has been urbanizing at a rapid rate since World War II; some part of the intermixture of developed and undeveloped land shown in figure 5 is due to the transitional nature of the area. As development

Figure 5. This map shows the intermixture of developed and undeveloped land in part of the New York SMSA at the end of 1964. The smallest used areas shown on the map are about 40 acres in size. As urbanization continues, some of the presently undeveloped land will be built upon, but some will still be idle some years from now.

proceeds, some of the presently undeveloped land will be built upon. However, all the information we have been able to obtain suggests that infilling is slow, and it seems highly probable that some of the areas that were idle at the end of 1964 will still be idle in 1974 and perhaps some in 1984.

The admixture of developed and undeveloped land shown in figure 5 is typical of many growing suburban areas and represents a form of "subdivision discontiguity." Builders obtain units of land and develop them as subdivisions; such units may vary from as little as 10 acres to a few hundred acres. Between the developed subdivisions lie tracts of various sizes and ownerships. Public services, such as water, sewers, roads, and schools, must ordinarily be extended to serve the entire area, and their costs per person or per household served are much higher than would be the case if the subdivisions were contiguous. The extent of these higher costs is imperfectly known and depends upon particular situations; we have estimated that the measurable public costs of subdivision discontiguity (for services such as noted above) average perhaps $150 per family annually for all families, to which would have to be added other sums for less easily measured public costs and for private costs such as greater travel cost.

In any discussion of the costs due to difference in "density" of land use, there is a considerable difference between subdivision contiguity (or its lack) and lot size or intensity of individual use of land. Some suburban residents may prefer large lots, and may be prepared to pay all the costs involved in them, the advantages of the large lot offsetting, in their minds, the extra costs. It is difficult to see any advantages from subdivision discontiguity. If the intervening vacant tracts were permanently set aside as open spaces for public use, then of course they would have value for this purpose and could be judged accordingly. However, this is precisely *not* the case; they are open for development, and will be developed whenever their owners and a developer can agree upon a price that each considers advantageous. The extra costs they impose on the tax-paying public are a price we have had to pay, thus far, for the form of the market in suburban land. The possibilities of a more rational use of land in and around our cities seem very great.

## EXTERNALITIES AND INTERDEPENDENCIES

The use and value of each piece of urban land is largely determined by activities on other tracts of land within the same urban area. If I live in a neighborhood that is drifting downhill, physically and socially, there is little or nothing that I can do to preserve the monetary value of my house or its value as a place to live. Likewise, if a neighborhood disintegrates, a retail store may start losing money.

In many instances, an individual is either harmed or benefited by what someone else does on the latter's own land. If my neighbor accumulates junk automobiles in his backyard until they become an eyesore, I have been harmed by his action; for whatever reason or benefit he collected the old autos, I have suffered. However, if he makes his backyard into a beautiful garden, clearly visible from my house, then I have gained. In one case, he took an action for which he did not pay all the costs and in the other case he did not get all the benefits. In both cases, there were what the economist calls an externality. Many externalities are negative—the smoke pouring out of a factory and inflicting soot on residents for many blocks is a classic example. There is a long legal history of such externalities—under what circumstances does the injured person have recourse in the form of monetary damages or to prevent the damaging action from continuing, and under what circumstances is it just too bad. But externalities can also be positive, as was shown in one of the examples.

I prefer to talk about interdependencies, rather than externalities. Although externalities and interdependencies are closely similar, I use interdependencies to connote a reciprocal relationship, rather than simply a causer and a recipient, and to connote that more than two parties are often involved. For instance, a group of businessmen, or of owners of undeveloped property, or of homeowners might jointly agree upon a renewal or building program in a neighborhood; each would incur costs and secure gains, but the gains would be larger for the whole group because the actions of each reinforced those of others.

In the modern world, the web of interdependencies in a city

grows more complicated and more important continuously. Air pollution is a notorious non-respecter of property lines. The losers from air pollution are very widely distributed, and come from all economic and social classes; likewise, the gainers from air pollution control or abatement are equally widely distributed. Water pollution may be equally serious and equally pervasive in its effect; water is more confined to predictable channels than air, and hence its pollution can sometimes be more readily avoided, at least by some people. But we all have an interest in the transportation system of a city—those who use it, and those whose homes are removed in order to build a new freeway. I have an interest that you should ride the subway so that the highway will be less congested when I want to drive—and vice versa.

Since economic values are involved in these interdependencies, one could well argue that there are property rights also. In some limited circumstances, such property rights have been recognized in the courts, as when neighbors sue to prevent certain uses of other residences or to prevent the construction of houses of nonconforming architecture. In general, however, both the economics and the law of urban interdependencies have been poorly developed. So, unfortunately, have been the social and political processes to reduce the negative externalities and to increase the positive ones. Land use zoning is a means of holding down negative externalities; it strives, with some success, to keep nonconforming uses out of a neighborhood. But it is not always effective here, and it is largely ineffective in promoting positive externalities. Zoning represents one intrusion upon the rights of fee simple ownership of land; society as a whole will not permit the landowner to do just anything he wishes with his land if it is judged that the adverse effects on others are unreasonably large. Zoning was bitterly opposed, in principle, by many people when it was first begun; it is still opposed bitterly in specific situations where it cramps the freedom of action of an individual. Any effort to increase positive externalities and to diminish negative ones in the cities of the future will almost certainly encounter resistance from those whose actions will be controlled or directed. The real problem is to find methods of social action that are effective in promoting the general welfare and that do not impose unreasonable restrictions upon the individual.

## DECISION-MAKING PROCESS FOR URBAN LAND

Who decides which urban land shall be used for each purpose, and which land shall be held vacant for some future use? The answer: everyone and, in the sense that everybody's business is nobody's business, no one. Many decisions about urban land use are made in a private market, but some are not. Even in a private transaction the buyer and seller operate within a social and governmental network; their decisions are influenced by zoning, subdivision codes, building and health codes, amounts and locations of many public services, and other conditioning factors. But they also operate within a complex private network; in particular, their decisions are influenced by estimates of land value that arise out of public reaction to various locations and land uses, supply and conditions of credit, presence or absence of competitors, and others. One of the most influential factors in many land transactions is federal tax law; the ability to treat gains in land value as a capital gain, normally subject to a lower tax rate than "ordinary income," is one factor; the ability to claim depreciation on an investment in an apartment house, regardless of how many prior owners have also secured depreciation on that same building, is another; still another is the ability of the homeowner to claim exemption for the interest and real estate taxes he has paid.

One of the most impressive aspects of the decision-making process is the number and variety of the actors. Landowners, land dealers, developers or builders, financial institutions, home buyers, and numerous agencies of government, especially of local government, are all involved. Each has some effect upon the use of land; each operates within a framework in which all the others are a major part; none has final responsibility for the overall result. If one does not like the suburbs that are built— and many have been highly critical of them—there is no single group or person who can be charged with the failure; if one seeks to change the suburbs of the future from those of the present, there is no single place where change can be made nor any single person whose decisions could change the process.

This complexity of decision making is only another way of emphasizing the interdependencies among the many residents of a modern urban agglomeration. Many people interact, in many ways. The decision-making process is intricate, not always fully understood, and full of inconsistencies and pockets of diverse action. A logical conclusion is that one should be wary of apparently simple proposals for change. A change in one factor—raising of the interest rate or tightening the terms of loans on homes, for instance—will have some effect upon the land use decisions of the whole urban complex. But the change may differ in degree or kind from what was intended; the anticipated effects may be partly avoided or offset or magnified by other actions of other actors. Moreover, there is a great inertia in urban land use; land use today depends more upon land use yesterday than upon any other single factor. Annual additions to housing stock are rarely as much as 3 percent of existing stock, for instance. It takes time, sometimes decades, to change many urban land uses.

If the urban society of the future is to plan its land use more carefully to achieve more of the positive externalities and to avoid more of the negative ones, then the complex decision-making processes of urban land use must be better understood than they have been in the past; and actions must usually be taken on a wide front rather than on single aspects of the decision-making process.

### An Appraisal of Suburbanization

The city (in the economic-physical sense of the term) has expanded in area in the United States in recent decades, whether one considers land used or land withdrawn. The expanding edge of the city is often called the suburb—a term that is imprecisely defined and variously used. Older suburbs may have expanded in area or new ones may have been built. In either case, the most extensive land use changes associated with cities in general have taken place in the suburbs. In 1970, according to some definitions of suburbs, more people lived in suburbs than in cities. In a great many ways, this is a suburban age, with suburban dwellers largely setting life styles for the whole population. Under these circumstances, one can scarcely refrain from making some evaluation of the suburbs in general. What have been their strengths and their weaknesses in contemporary American life? One would expect something as nearly universal as the suburb to be both strongly criticized and warmly defended, and this has indeed been the case.

Criticisms of suburbs built after World War II have fallen mostly into three categories:

1. The suburbanization process has operated to exclude the poor and the nonwhite. Indeed, this is one aspect of suburban growth on which a preponderant majority of the numerous decision makers mentioned above could agree. A number of measures have often been employed to bring about this result. Not only have large lot sizes made land costly and low-priced housing impossible, but various other measures have been designed to provide a restrictive type of population growth for suburbs. The overtly racial actions are now illegal, but the barriers are not wholly down. Even if there had been no deliberate effort to exclude both poor and nonwhite groups, the costliness of most suburban housing would have worked to this end. A full half, or more, of the total population is effectively excluded from suburban living because they cannot afford to buy the only kind of new housing available there.

2. The suburban housing that has been produced is too costly in terms of what it does provide. As noted above, discontiguity in subdivisions in suburban areas has added to the cost of public services by about $150 annually per suburban family. But this figure excludes extra transportation costs for the family, extra highway costs outside the suburbs necessitated by the greater auto travel to job centers, extra air pollution as a result of such travel, and numerous other public and private costs. To the costs due to subdivision discontiguity must be added other costs due to large lot sizes and to low intensity of lot utilization. With

costly land sites, the development of lower-priced suburban housing has been nearly impossible.

3. The typical suburb is aesthetically unattractive. Much harsh criticism has been directed at suburbs on this ground. I do not pretend to special competence in this field, hence make no judgment about the typical suburban architecture. I have been impressed, however, with the typical builder's bulldozing of his site, destroying all trees and other vegetation that interfere with his building process; the homeowner then has the expensive and often frustrating experience of replacing trees and other vegetation. The race is to see if the trees will be big enough to support a hammock by the time the mortgage is paid off.

Though the critics have dwelt on these and other aspects of suburban growth, the modern American suburb has had its defenders—or, perhaps one should say, its glorifiers. Of the many arguments in praise of typical suburbs, two seem to have importance:

1. The typical suburb built in the past 20 years has provided the basis for comfortable living. The houses have a wide range of the newest gadgets, they can be kept warm in winter and cool in summer, they provide a large amount of space for the average family (the idea of a separate bedroom for each child is now rather firmly established—a goal of personal space unattainable in most of the world today and in this country in my youth), and the interior at least may have a considerable measure of charm. Since other families of similar age, income, and interests are attracted to the same area, there can be congenial friends and social institutions. This type of argument contrasts the suburb with the older apartment, which would sometimes be the practical alternative for the same families, and the suburb comes out ahead by a large margin.

2. The way in which the suburbanization process has worked for the past two decades or more has brought forth the ingenuity and resourcefulness of a large private building sector, and in the process enough housing has been built to supply those who can afford it. This type of argument contrasts the private-

builder approach with a public-housing approach, and the suburb wins again.

The suburbs built since World War II do indeed have many good points. Probably the best way of summing up the situation is to say that they might readily have been better.

## RENEWAL OF OLDER CITY AREAS

One important land use shift within the cities has been the renewal or rebuilding of the older city areas—or, more accurately, the lag in such rebuilding. In many an American city, the residential area of its early years, when the city was small, has long since deteriorated badly. When cities were small in population and in area, and were growing fast in both ways, an active demand for land for commercial, industrial, apartment, and other uses would often lead to the private rebuilding of the older residential areas. Moreover, if an area was ceasing to be attractive for residential living because of changes in land use on surrounding tracts, it did not much matter if a house was allowed to deteriorate—it would be replaced anyway. But, as cities grow older and larger, their rate of growth usually becomes too slow to provide a market for all the land in older housing to be transformed into other land uses. As noted earlier, residential use of land, including streets within residential areas, is by far the largest use of land within cities; a modest annual obsolescence of housing within this large area is likely to release far more land than even a rapid rate of growth in commercial and other land uses can absorb.

Rebuilding of decadent residential areas with new housing has not proceeded rapidly in many cities. For one thing, U.S. income tax laws have often favored the retention of slum rental dwellings as such. Each owner can charge off depreciation and have a tax-free cash flow for some years. If he sells the property for more than his tax basis (which is the price he paid for property *minus* the depreciation he has taken) the profit is taxed as a capital gain at a lower tax rate; if he suffers a loss, he can charge it against his other income. The process can be repeated by subsequent purchasers without limit. In spite of this, in many cities today much slum residential property has become derelict and abandoned; mortgaged to the hilt; too run-down to meet health code standards; and, with local real estate taxes delinquent, the title may not be clear. Such property does not offer an attractive investment possibility to any investor. For the more favorably located such areas, it may be profitable to tear down old buildings, and to replace them with new luxury high-rise apartments; this is happening in some parts of many cities. But this neither meets the needs of the low-income residents of such areas nor offers a solution for all the deteriorating older residential property—the market for luxury apartments is simply not sufficiently extensive.

In an attempt to improve this situation, a program of public urban renewal was initiated some years ago. Those who criticize the program point out that the renewal process is slow, with clear land sometimes standing idle for years; that low-income families are displaced, and similar conditions soon arise somewhere else; that large subsidies are required, which benefit present landowners and new users of the area, neither of whom is in need of such public subsidy; and that only a small fraction of the areas needing renewal are reached by public programs. The urban renewal program has had its defenders, but few people have been fully satisfied with it. Perhaps its greatest accomplishment has been to provide a striking demonstration of how difficult the renewal process really is.

One of the major unsolved problems of urban land use is how to secure an orderly and socially acceptable rebuilding of decaying residential areas.

## THE FUTURE OF URBAN LAND USE

Every responsible student or observer of current affairs expects a larger population in the United States in the decades ahead. Family planning may become universal and fully effective at some future date, but it will take some time to achieve this, and in the meantime population will continue to grow. The large numbers of young people in the population today will lead to large further increases even if the birthrate should fall to a level that would ultimately produce a constant population. An atomic war might change this outlook, so most forecasters hedge by excluding such wars. The real issues are the rate of population growth and the level, if any, at which further growth stops and the population levels off. Birthrates in the United States have varied greatly in the past; in the 1960s, for example, they fell dramatically. Long-term projections of population necessarily involve some assumption as to future birthrates and often seem to be greatly influenced by recent variations in the birthrate. For instance, just a few years ago, virtually every analyst was speaking of 300 million or more people by 2000; by the late 1960s, estimates were coming down somewhat, and the 300 million figure for 2000 seems more like an upper limit.

In many ways, it does not matter what the precise projection is for any future date; we assume that the trend is upward, at least for a generation, and at a net rate of annual increase of one percent or more. Someday—if not in the year 2000, then perhaps a decade or so later—we will probably reach 300 million total population.

If trends of the past generation or more continue, then nearly all the net increase in population will live in urban agglomerations—within cities in the physical-economic sense, if not in the legal-political sense. Thus, there will be a greater proportionate increase in urban population than in total population. If 73 percent of the 204 million people in 1970 lived in "urban" areas, as these were then defined, and if the nonurban population does not rise, then somewhat more than 80 percent of the population will live in similar urban areas when the total population reaches 300 million. For this number of urban people there will have to be more land in urban agglomerations.

Changes in the number, area, and population of cities since 1800 are shown in figure 6. Data for past changes are far from perfect, but this chart uses the best data available. The projections to 2000 should not be taken too literally; the actual course of affairs may be somewhat different, especially if total population growth is different than assumed. But the general relationships are, I believe, correct. They provide a basis for

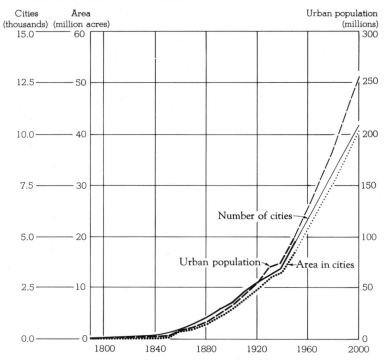

Cities           Area                                    Urban population
(thousands) (million acres)                                  (millions)

**Figure 6.** This chart illustrates the changes that have taken place and are likely to take place in the number, area, and population of cities in the United States. Although the data are far from perfect, the general relationships are believed to be correct, and they provide the factual basis for the frequently heard statement that from 1960 to 2000 the United States will build as much new urban development as it now has.

the frequent assertion that the United States from 1960 to 2000 will build as much urban development as it had built in its entire history up to 1960. Moreover, actual building will be greater than this, because some of the present houses and other structures are so old that they must be replaced.

The amount of land that will be required to accommodate this future urban growth depends upon the form of the future city. If growth were to be wholly in single-family houses, each upon its own large lot, then relatively a lot of land would be required; in 1960, most analysts of the urban scene would have projected primary dependence upon the single-family home. In the 1960s, however, there was a marked resurgence of apartment building, and in some years apartments accounted for half of all new dwelling units. Was this a temporary phenomenon or was it the beginning of a trend that will see a still larger reliance on apartments? As with birthrate and population projections, long-term projections of urban land use seem to rest heavily on recent trends. Apartment houses in the past have required much less land for a given number of people than single family houses. This may be less true in the future; some of the recent apartment house building has been in suburban locations, and the apartments have been surrounded by extensive open areas, including golf courses and other recreation and scenic areas.

The amount of land withdrawn for urban uses in the future, from other land uses, depends in large measure upon the extent of idle land within the urban complexes—upon subdivision contiguity or its lack. In several metropolitan areas, the amount of idle land within the presently urbanized areas (as these have been defined by the Bureau of the Census) could accommodate growth for two decades or longer. If infilling of presently idle land should become general, then the total area over which urban development was spread would be much less than if present subdivision discontiguity continued.

Future urban development will probably occur reasonably near the present larger urban developments (figure 7). While it may be argued that future locational forces will differ from past ones, it is also true that inertia is a powerful force. It is often easier to expand a present city, especially by relatively modest increments, than to build a new one. The home builder can sell to people who have jobs in the existing city; the employer can find a labor force from among the existing population; there need not be a precise correlation between job expansion and housing expansion, although they cannot get very far out of adjustment without serious consequences. Likewise, there need not be a precise correlation between consumers and retail trade centers, nor between population and school facilities; some flexibility, within some limits, is possible.

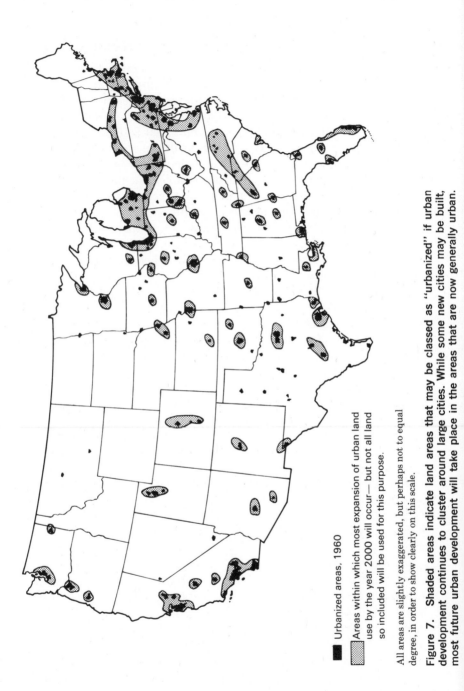

■ Urbanized areas, 1960

▨ Areas within which most expansion of urban land
use by the year 2000 will occur — but not all land
so included will be used for this purpose.

All areas are slightly exaggerated, but perhaps not to equal
degree, in order to show clearly on this scale.

Figure 7.  Shaded areas indicate land areas that may be classed as "urbanized" if urban
development continues to cluster around large cities. While some new cities may be built,
most future urban development will take place in the areas that are now generally urban.

Much of this expansion will take the form of new suburbs, or of large suburban subdivisions that are in themselves essentially suburbs. Even if some rather large modifications are made in the processes of urban growth—and the prospects are far from great that they will be—the suburb will continue to be a major form of urban expansion.

What about "new towns"? The answer depends in part upon whether one means a satellite city or a free-standing one.

A satellite new town would be located close enough to an existing city or metropolis for the people who live in one to work in the other, and the new town's life would be rather closely interwoven with the life of the larger center, in spite of some physical separation. The problems and opportunities of a satellite new town are rather similar to those of a large suburb; the differences are more in degree than in kind. Some satellite new towns might be developed by private business, although these are large enterprises that take a lot of capital, and thus far they have not shown a capacity to earn profits commensurate with the risk.

A free-standing new town would probably be located farther from a major city; economic ties would be weak, and commuting would be nearly impossible. The need to balance housing, jobs, commercial services, and public services at each state of development makes the free-standing new town an extremely difficult undertaking. The town must not only offer a reasonable prospect of such balance when fully developed; it must also provide a reasonable balance from the beginning and at every stage. If the developer erects houses faster than jobs develop, he will have difficulty in selling the houses; if an industry moves in before a labor force is resident, it will experience a labor shortage. Moreover, the balance must be by skills and occupations. A shopping district that is designed to serve the ultimate population well is likely to be largely idle (and depressing) during the earlier development years, whereas one that is designed to serve the early population may experience severe difficulty in expanding to meet the long-term needs.

My own opinion is that relatively few self-standing new towns can or will be built unless a national policy to assist them is adopted. One necessary part of such a policy, I believe, must be public acquisition of the land area needed; the land could then be sold or leased for long periods to private developers as they needed it. Such a program of public land acquisition would not, alone, ensure success of the self-standing new towns; their developers would need a lot of other help, public or private, especially access to ample capital. To be successful, such towns would have to be well located, well planned, and efficiently developed. The idea of new towns has aroused much interest, even excitement, but the difficulties must be faced frankly or the idea is likely to be discredited by early failure.

# CHAPTER FOUR

# Land for Recreation

Mass participation in outdoor recreation on the scale now practiced in the United States is a relatively new development. Total visits to all units of the national park system are now about equal to the total number of people in the country; those who visit two or more parks and those who go at least twice to the same park about offset the considerable number of persons who never visit any area. Total visits to national forests are also about equal to total population. Total visits to all reservoirs constructed by the Corps of Engineers considerably exceed total population, and total visits to state parks are more than double total population. The average person makes one visit annually to some unit of the national park system, one to a national forest, one to a Corps reservoir, two to a state park, an unknown number but perhaps half a dozen or more to a city park, and unknown but substantial numbers to other public areas and to private areas. To do this, consumers in the United States spend many billions of dollars annually for recreation equipment, transportation equipment, travel, and the other necessary costs of outdoor recreation. Moreover, all of this has been growing rapidly and steadily for many years, and shows no signs of slackening in rate of growth. These are the manifestations of mass outdoor recreation.

In the past, the average citizen had neither the income nor the leisure to engage in outdoor recreation on this scale, nor were there likely to be areas set aside specifically for recreation to which he could go. Mass outdoor recreation is both a reflection of a new life style emerging in the United States and an important component of that life style. It is possible only because of the high productivity of our economic system.

Outdoor recreation is a rising use of land and water in the

United States today; it can often compete against other potential uses of land, both in terms of the value of its output and in the political arena. The importance of the land used for recreation purposes stems from its location and the number of persons involved. Compared with the land used by the "big three" of grazing, forestry, and cropland, the total acreage of land in recreation use is small—about 40 million acres in the 48 contiguous states and less than 50 million in all 50 states. But the number of people rather directly concerned is large—perhaps more than half the population, the exact number is not known—and the locational requirements of recreation land are often critical. A city park, for instance, needs only a small percentage of the land in the residential district it serves, but it must be located within easy reach of the people in that area if it is to be usable at all. Recreation differs from the "big three" in another way: as a land use, it is a form of consumption not of production. The farmer produces wheat, the recreationist consumes outdoor recreation.

### THE OUTDOOR RECREATION EXPERIENCE

Basic to any understanding of the land requirements for outdoor recreation is an understanding of the physical, economic, and psychological aspects of the whole recreation experience, which consists of five more or less clearly separate phases: anticipation, travel to, on site, travel back, and recollection. Each of these is present in every outdoor recreation experience, though their relative importance may vary greatly.

*Anticipation* is the planning stage of an outdoor recreation experience. It takes place in the recreationist's home town, usually in his own home. This is when he decides where to go, when, with what equipment, for what specific activities, which members of the family will go, how long they will stay, how much they can afford to spend, and all the rest of it. The planning may be careful and methodical, based upon ample accurate data; or it may be impressionistic, uninformed, mere wishful thinking; or it may be something intermediate. This is perhaps the most important stage of the whole experience, for what takes place later all has its origins here—even though plans may not work out exactly. This is also the phase when special equipment, gasoline, and groceries are bought and half of all the costs are incurred.

*Travel to* the actual recreation site is also necessary, unless one has the necessary facilities in his own backyard. This travel may be short, as to a neighborhood playground or a city park; or it may be extremely long, as when one visits a national park across the country; or it may be intermediate in length. For most outdoor recreation activities, travel to the site requires an appreciable proportion of the total time spent on the whole experience; often as much time is spent in travel as at the site itself. Monetary costs are also considerable. Attitudes toward travel seem to be mixed: many people report sightseeing and travel as the chief attraction in their outdoor recreation experiences; others see travel as an unattractive but necessary part of the experience.

*On site* experiences are those commonly thought of in connection with outdoor recreation. They run the gamut of specific activities—organized sports of all kinds, hunting and fishing, camping and picnicking, the variety of water sports, all sorts of specialized activities such as rock climbing and cave exploration, and much just plain resting and loafing. For some purposes, it is possible to group all these activities together as outdoor recreation; but, to the park or playground administrator as well as to the participant, each separate activity presents its own requirements, problems, and rewards. For the general outdoor recreation experience, participation is often on a family basis, and a variety of activities to appeal to different age and sex groups is essential.

*Travel back* is in some ways the counterpart of travel to the area, but it may have important differences. The routes need not be the same, nor the time spent, nor even the money spent. Perhaps most important of all, the recreationist and his family may approach this travel in a different spirit than they did travel to the site. Little is known about attitudes to travel either way, and still less about differences according to the direction of the travel.

*Recollection* is the last of the major phases. Like the first, it takes place primarily in the recreationist's home town, in his home or office or in the homes of his friends. It may be supplemented by pictures taken on the trip, or by souvenirs brought back. It may bear little relationship to what actually happened—the fish get bigger, the mosquitoes get more numerous, or the athletic exploits get more outstanding. But no small part of the payoff of the whole experience takes place here; it is the memories that people carry with them that determine whether they will go back. Recollection of one experience gradually merges with planning for the next.

These five phases of outdoor recreation form a package—a package of costs that must be considered, a package of results that must be balanced against the costs. No one element of cost can be considered independently of the others. It does not help if the entrance fee is low or even free, if other costs are high; people are likely to remember and to gripe about having to pay an unreasonably high price for a cup of coffee. Magnificent scenery in the park may long be remembered, but so may dirty rest rooms at the service stations en route. All aspects of the whole experience add together to provide a range and variety of pleasurable experiences; all costs of the whole experience also add together, and must be more than offset by the advantages if the user is to repeat the experience.

In considering ways to improve the total recreation experience, attention should be directed to all phases, not merely to the on-site phase. In my judgment, the greatest opportunity for improvement of the outdoor recreation experience lies in the two travel phases. Our modern highways are mostly fast, comfortable, and safe; but the average traveller has little idea of what he is seeing or what it means. Signs and maps show him how to get from one city to another, or from one point on a map to another. But no one has ever been much concerned with what he saw or what he thought about what he saw. The new interstate superhighways are particularly bad in this regard; one can travel them with almost nothing to indicate what state, region, or locality he is in—New England, Middle West, South, and Far West all look alike. It should be possible to devise practical attractive means of involving the traveller's mind as well as his body. Well-written little leaflets, roadside radio broadcasts that could be picked up only within a radius of a few miles, and recorded tapes that could be played back within the car are among the devices that might be made available to travellers who want to be informed about geology, geography, forests, agriculture, industry, history, government, and other aspects of the local countryside through which they are travelling. If the broadcasts were offered as an option, they would not disturb those who prefer the latest songs or baseball games on the radio, and they might delight those who travel in hopes of learning something. Programs of this sort might be undertaken by government agencies, either federal, state, or local; or by private firms—there seems to be no more reason for private firms not undertaking these programs than there is for them being the principal suppliers of road maps; or by a combination of public research and writing with private business provision of the necessary service. The typical park or recreation agency has not thought about aspects of the recreation experience outside the site it administers, and the typical highway department has not concerned itself with such matters.

The whole experience is a useful concept in considering the economics of outdoor recreation also, and thus the area of land used for this purpose. "Costs" can be expressed in dollars, in time, and in travel distance; all three are involved. For much outdoor recreation, these three measures will be highly correlated. That is, a long trip measured in miles is also likely to be a costly one measured in dollars, and to require a relatively long time. Conversely, a trip for a short distance is likely to cost a lot less money and to take much less time. If these three measures were invariably in the same relationship to one another, any one of them could be used as a measure for all three; and, since costs are usually thought of in monetary terms, dollars would do to measure miles and time as well.

However, these measures of cost are not invariably correlated; also, one kind of cost can substitute for another to some extent. One can think of situations where money costs are moderate but time costs large; a canoe trip may fall into this category. Or one may think of an expensive outdoor recreation experience that does not involve too much travel or time. Moreover, the kind of cost that will limit outdoor recreation activities will differ considerably, depending upon the circumstances of the individual. For the family whose money income is low, money costs are likely to be the most seriously limiting factor; for the man whose annual income is high, limitations of time are likely to be more restrictive. However, a man can stretch his time by using some of his money; he can, for instance, fly from his home city to an airport relatively near his vacation objective, and there rent a car, thus saving hours or days of driving. Likewise, the man with relatively high income may install air conditioning or otherwise add to the comfort of his travel by car, assuming that he chooses to go that way.

I have spoken of costs as if they were obviously and uniquely observable and measurable. In fact, costs fall into different categories. The immediate cash costs of a particular recreation trip are one thing; the total costs, including replacement of equipment, may be much larger. When the family owns an auto capable of making the desired trip, and when it owns the various kinds of specialized equipment required, then cash costs may be low—limited to gasoline, food, and other direct expenditures. A family's first camping trip will be relatively far more expensive than later trips until the time comes when all equipment must be replaced. The full costs of outdoor recreation must be met sooner or later, but not necessarily for each trip at the time. In planning its recreation activities, the family is perhaps influenced more by the immediate than by the long-run costs. However, in judging between two alternative sites or programs, it may well be that the ratio between direct costs is not much different than the ratio between total costs.

The whole outdoor recreation experience must be looked at in psychological terms as well. What effect did it have on the persons who went? Was it mildly pleasurable, or deeply moving, or boring, or unpleasant in some way? If the family, or some other group, travelled together, did the members of the group have similar or diverse reactions? What about the reactions of each member of the group toward the others in the group, and how were these affected by any aspect of the physical and economic experience?

Perhaps a more basic set of questions is concerned with what people sought from the outdoor recreation experience. Were they trying to escape an unsatisfactory situation at home, or to escape from the company of others? Someone has characterized some outdoor recreation experiences as "unfun"—undertaken not in the expectation of any real enjoyment but because they are less unpleasant than the alternative use of time. Some men are said to go on fishing and hunting trips to avoid their wives, for instance. Was the recreation experience visualized primarily in terms of sheer enjoyment? Or was the participant desirous of proving to someone, perhaps to himself, that he had the ability to climb a mountain, hike on a mountain trail, canoe in a lake or river, or otherwise do something out of his ordinary routine? Does the recreationist want to get away from people or be where other people are? What does he consider good neighborliness and what is crowding?

To this matter of what the recreationist sought can be added another range of questions: What did he perceive? As he wandered among the redwoods, was he awed and stirred by their height and majesty, or was he conscious of toilet paper littering the ground? Or were his thoughts back on the delicious or the unsatisfactory meal he had at the restaurant down the road? The Smithsonian Institution, in a recent release, tells the story of a conversation overheard between two women visitors: "Where did you go on your vacation?" "Went to the Cayman Islands." "Where in the world are they?" "I haven't the least idea. We flew." There is good reason to suspect that a great many visitors at many outdoor recreation areas do not really understand what they are seeing; they might as well have gone elsewhere or stayed home.

Still other questions might be raised about the psychological aspects of a recreation experience. For those who had a reasonably good idea of what they sought, and sufficient perception to understand and appreciate what they experienced, was this an efficient place or way in which to get the psychological experience that he or they sought? Some persons and some families are highly experienced in outdoor recreation, know where they like to go and what they want to do, and make reasoned and efficient choices. But there is reason to suspect that a substantial proportion of the population has only vague ideas about what it really wants, and still vaguer ideas about where to get it. Many are swayed by advertising or are motivated by the desire to show that they have been to an "in" place; they enjoy the car window or bumper sticker more than they do the trip. One of the missing elements in the outdoor recreation scene is a place or an institution where the uninformed person can get accurate and useful information on a wide range of outdoor recreation activities and sites. Travel agents, airlines, steamship companies, and others advertise such services, but they nearly always are oriented toward the services they are prepared to perform.

Enjoyment of an outdoor recreation experience is also affected by crowding, which is as much a reflection of the individual's perception of the physical situation as it is of the situation itself. Some people like to visit with others in a recreation area, sharing experiences and opinions; and some go along with the old saw that a campground is comfortably full when a man can use his neighbor's tent stakes for his own. Park management personnel have often seen campers crowd up in one end of a campground when there was room for them to spread out. Crowding is perhaps best defined as a situation where the individual receives more sensory perceptions than he can handle. Some have a low tolerance, at least at some time, and want privacy and solitude.

SOCIOECONOMIC FACTORS UNDERLYING OUTDOOR RECREATION

The mass outdoor recreation activity of the United States rests on several major socioeconomic factors: income, leisure, personal characteristics of the individuals, and certain social characteristics.

The effect of income is both national and personal. Differences in national income affect the ability of a nation, a state, or a city to provide outdoor recreation areas, to improve them, to provide transportation facilities so that users can reach them, and to produce the specialized goods and services involved in outdoor recreation. The rising trend in economic output in the United States (somewhat obscured or confused by economic fluctuations and by rising prices) is well known, and need not be described here. In spite of many competing demands for governmental revenues, the federal, state, and local governments have been able to afford extensions of the existing park systems in recent years—not as rapidly as park supporters would like, not perhaps as rapidly as would be economically most efficient, but nevertheless substantial additions. The highway and air networks, developed partly for business transportation, serve the recreation needs quite well. Some highways have been built primarily to serve outdoor recreation areas; on some highways, peak recreation traffic flows exceed weekday work flows, and highways have to be designed to meet these recreation peak flows. Some airlines have developed a lot of business flying recreationists to resort areas in both winter and summer. The production of automobiles for outdoor recreation is a major undertaking; station wagons, campers, trailers, and other special equipment are designed partly or wholly for outdoor recreation use. Boats, motors, and other special equipment are manufactured to provide the means for water sports. A very wide range of equipment is designed for the camping family; manufacture of sports equipment is big business; and in other ways the productive capacity of American industry serves outdoor recreation.

Personal income also affects participation in outdoor recreation. As everyone knows from his own experience, it costs money to travel to recreation sites and to buy the necessary or desired equipment. Studies of groups of people show that the proportion who participate in outdoor recreation rises as average incomes rise, and that the amount of outdoor recreation activity per person also rises with higher incomes. Although some high-income persons or families do not engage in outdoor recreation, or do so only sparingly, and some lower-income people do so a great deal, there is on the average a considerable relationship between personal income and the extent of outdoor recreation activity. Perhaps more than the total amount of recreation activity, the kind of such activity is influenced by income. Yachts are hardly for the family with a moderate or low income, to use an extreme example. But travel to an African national park to see its spectacular game animals is relatively expensive, as is a mountain-climbing expedition far from home. On the other hand, some forms of outdoor recreation are relatively inexpensive. For instance, the family that owns an automobile may go for a picnic with little additional cost for food or transportation.

Where a person goes for outdoor recreation is also influenced by his income. Closer areas are nearly always cheaper to visit than more distant ones, hence persons with limited income tend to travel shorter distances. But public areas are cheaper than owning one's own summer or winter vacation spot. Attendance at public outdoor recreation areas rises with average family income, up to a level that might be described as somewhat above average; as incomes rise further, attendance at public areas does not increase further.

The amount, timing, and sizes of pieces of leisure affect the amount, location, and kinds of outdoor recreation. There has been a good deal of confusion about leisure, and the term itself does not have an unequivocal meaning. Some time is required for existence—sleeping, eating, some personal chores, and the like; other time is required for subsistence—work, travel to and from work, school for young people, housework for the housewife, and so on. Beyond these, time may be used for various purposes; the broadest definition of leisure is all time not required for existence and subsistence. Leisure time may be filled to the brim, and over, with activities. The person who has so many social, personal hobby, and public service activities that he is harried for time is similar to the person who has committed his discretionary income to monthly installment payments for a range of consumer goods until he lacks spending money—indeed, may be the same person. Thus, leisure is not idleness; it may be doubted if much idleness is true leisure, but may more appropriately be considered "non-time," mere time killing or time wasting. It is altogether possible that the rise in leisure, described below, has been accompanied by a still greater increase in demand for time, so that the mythical average person has less uncommitted time today than his father or grandfather had.

In the typical American household, there is a little leisure between rising and departure for work or school—time to read at least part of the morning newspaper, or for some visiting with other members of the family. There may be leisure intervals during the day—coffee breaks at the office, recess at school, coffee klatches for the housewife. In the late afternoon and evening, there are some hours for leisure activities. These are various forms of daily leisure. Then there is weekend leisure—much more time on Saturday and Sunday for doing what one chooses. Holidays at intervals and vacation time, once a year or scattered through the year, provide an opportunity for activities different from those typical of either daily or weekend leisure. Young people, not yet in the labor force, and retired persons who have withdrawn from the labor force have still other patterns of leisure.

Over the past two or three generations, the amount of each of these kinds of outdoor recreation has risen. Hours of work per day have fallen, as have days of work per week; at the end of World War I, for instance, the hours of work in the steel industry were 12 hours a day, seven days a week—a brutal working schedule, with little time or energy for recreation. The paid vacation was rather uncommon before World War II; today, it is standard for most employment, and has grown longer over time. Young people once began to work at 13, 14, or 15; today, compulsory school attendance laws keep nearly all of them in school past 16 years, most of them past 18 years, and a rising appreciation of the value of education keeps half or more of them in school until 22 years or more. In an earlier day, few people could afford to retire as long as they were physically able to work. Today, a combination of public and private retirement plans, plus some extension of the average life span, has greatly increased the years in retirement from an average of three years in 1900 to six years today and an estimated nine years by 2000. The combination of increases in various forms of leisure and increases in total population has led to the national total hours of leisure rising from 177 billion in 1900 to 453 billion in 1950 and to an expected level of 1,113 billion by 2000.

Since the rise in leisure has been less than the rise in real income per capita, many persons are able to afford the money for some activity, but not the time, and a variety of time-money tradeoffs have developed. Some people will fly to a vacation area and rent a car, rather than drive; the money cost may be greater, but the time saving is substantial. Some choose to belong to a private tennis club, at considerable cost, rather than to play on public courts where they will have a long wait for a court. The number and variety of time-saving devices will probably increase, even though they add to the money cost of outdoor recreation.

Various personal factors also affect participation in outdoor recreation activity. For instance, total recreation activity tends to decline with age, and participation by those over 65 averages not much more than half of that for those 18 to 24 years of age. There are great differences among individuals in this respect, of course. There are also differences among specific outdoor recreation activities. Swimming is an activity primarily for the young, while walking for pleasure increases as an activity with older persons. One must be careful about attributing all these differences in rates of participation among persons of different ages in the present population to the aging factor. For instance, at the time when the older people were young, swimming was less popular and in many areas there were no facilities where one could swim; and walking was far more of a recreation activity a few decades ago than it is today. When the young people of the present are old, will they swim more, and walk less, than the present older generation? In other words, how much of the observed difference in participation rates associated with age is due to a difference in life styles of the generations involved, and how much is due to the aging process itself? Only time can provide a reliable answer.

Sex affects participation in outdoor recreation somewhat—less for total participation than for kinds of recreation. Hunting, fishing, mountain climbing, and some sports are participated in much more by men than by women. Some activities, as picnicking, are dominantly family activities. There are other age and sex patterns of outdoor recreation activity.

Race has affected outdoor recreation activity in the past and blacks have generally not participated in activities such as water sports and camping to the same extent as whites, even when allowance is made for differences in income. As racial discrimination is reduced, these differences will probably decline.

Outdoor recreation activity is also affected by education; it rises with increased education. However, there are differences among outdoor activities in this regard. A disproportionately large proportion of those visiting wilderness areas have had a college education or have done postgraduate work, for instance. The increase in outdoor recreation activity is particularly marked as education increases up to the level of high school completion; above that, further education has little net effect upon total outdoor recreation activity.

Occupation has some effect on outdoor recreation, the latter rising as occupations go up a scale toward managerial and professional. Laborers and unskilled workers participate a great deal less. Again, there are differences among the forms of outdoor recreation; hunting is dominantly a sport of blue-collar workers.

All of the foregoing are net relationships; the effect of each factor is measured with the others held constant. When several of these factors are combined, their effect is greater. For instance, a young, high-income, professional man, with paid vacation, will likely partake of a lot more outdoor recreation than a low-income, aged farmer. The latter is likely to take his shotgun and go rabbit hunting; he is most unlikely to take a long trip to a distant national park. The professional man has the income to partake of both a wide variety and a large amount of outdoor recreation.

However, all of these effects apply to rather large groups. Knowing the characteristics of a group permits one to estimate the proportion of the group that will partake of outdoor recreation in general and of particular kinds of outdoor recreation, and to estimate rather accurately the total volume of such recreation activity. But this knowledge does not provide a reliable basis for forecasting what a particular individual will do. Personal taste enters here, and apparently is a major determinant. Two men of the same age, with the same education and occupation, the same income and leisure, and living in the same neighborhood, may have very different patterns of outdoor recreation; one may never go to a recreation area, the other may go often and engage in a wide range of specific activities. Thus far, we have found no way to predict accurately just what a particular individual will do; we can only say that, if he is a member of a group that consumes a lot of recreation, he is probably active in outdoor recreation. But he may not be. These differences in individual taste may stem from some element in the early or family lives of the persons concerned, but we lack any real understanding of the factors affecting personal taste in outdoor recreation.

PARK SYSTEMS

The increased demand for recreational use of land has made planning and operating parks a big business. Public areas, referred to simply as "parks" in this section, include: national parks, national monuments, national seashores, national recreation areas, national forests, federal wildlife refuges, state parks (which in themselves have a score or more of specialized names), state forests, state game refuges, regional parks, city parks, city playgrounds, and scores of other areas with specialized names that reflect their histories or legal authorization.

As an aid to managing parks, the Outdoor Recreation Resources Review Commission (ORRRC) proposed a sixfold classification of outdoor recreation areas that is coming to be used by many park planners and administrators. Class I areas are high-density recreation areas, characterized by a high degree of facility development, used exclusively for recreation, suitable for a wide range of activities, and particularly suited for day and weekend use. They are generally located close to or within major centers of population. Class II areas are general outdoor recreation areas, involving more extensive and less crowded uses for a large and varied amount of activity; emphasis is upon the natural setting. Such areas are popular for day, weekend, and vacation use. Class III areas are natural environment areas; emphasis is upon leaving the natural environment as unchanged as possible, with recreation activities compatible with such environment; some such areas are used exclusively for recreation, but many also support forest production, grazing, or other land uses. Improvements on such areas are kept to the minimum that will meet the needs of visitors. Class IV areas are the unique natural areas—remarkable natural wonders, areas of high scenic splendor, or of scientific importance; preservation of these natural resources in their natural condition is the primary management objective. These areas are limited in number, because of their demanding characteristics; they are, or should be, used only for a particular type of outdoor recreation, and are mostly located where they can be visited only during vacations. Class V are the primitive areas, with no commercial utilization or mechanical transportation; they must be large enough to give the visitor the sense that he is enjoying a wilderness experience. Class VI are national historic and cultural sites that merit preservation.

Another classification—and one that lends itself to planning the number, kind, and location of outdoor recreation areas—is shown in table 3, and discussed below. In this system, the criteria are primarily economic ones, and distance is a prime consideration. As noted earlier, distance is usually correlated with time and/or money costs, and hence has a decided influence on the use that is made of a recreation area.

*User-oriented outdoor recreation areas* must be located close to where people live. The playground, city park, local swimming pool, tennis courts, and golf courses are good examples of this kind of area. People use them primarily after work or after school, although mothers with small children and elderly people may use them during the day. The individual areas or tracts for this kind of outdoor recreation need not be large—anywhere from a few to perhaps 100 to 200 acres will serve in most cases. Land characteristics are not particularly demanding, although moderately level sites, fairly well drained, and not subject to too serious flooding, are preferable. Wherever people live, they will want recreation areas of this general type; unless the areas can

TABLE 3. GENERAL CLASSIFICATION OF OUTDOOR RECREATIONAL USES AND RESOURCES

| Item | Type of recreation area | | |
|------|-------------|----------------|--------------|
| | User-oriented | Resource-based | Intermediate |
| General location | Close to users; on whatever resources are available | Where outstanding resources can be found; may be distant from most users | Must not be too remote from users; on best resources available within distance limitation |
| Major types of activity | Games, such as golf and tennis; swimming; picnicking; walks and horse riding; zoos, etc.; playing by children | Major sightseeing; scientific and historical interest; hiking and mountain climbing; camping, fishing, and hunting | Camping, picnicking, hiking, swimming, hunting, fishing |
| When major use occurs | After hours (school or work) | Vacations | Day outings and weekends |
| Typical sizes of areas | One to a hundred, or at most to a few hundred acres | Usually some thousands of acres, perhaps many thousands | A hundred to several thousand acres |
| Common types of agency responsibility | City, county, or other local government; private | National parks and national forests primarily; state parks in some cases; private, especially for seashore and major lakes | State parks; private |

Source: Marion Clawson, R. Burnell Held, and Charles H. Stoddard, Land for the Future (Baltimore: The Johns Hopkins Press for Resources for the Future, 1962).

be conveniently located, they are useless to the people concerned. For instance, a playground must usually lie within half a mile of its users, and there must be a safe route from home to playground.

Resource-based outdoor recreation areas lie at the other end of the scale. Here it is the superb natural features of the area that are dominant. Mountains, sea and lake shores, deserts, swamps, and other unusual natural landscapes fall in this category. Such areas are where you find them; man may protect them and make them available for users, but he cannot make them—he can do much to destroy their attractiveness. Most of these areas lie at considerable distances from where most people live. Accordingly, considerable travel, with attendant costs, is involved in visiting such areas. As a result, they are visited primarily during annual vacations. Some such areas are in federal ownership, as national parks, national monuments, or national forests; a few state parks qualify for this category; and some such areas are in private ownership. Individual tracts are often large, sometimes with a million acres or more.

*Intermediate outdoor recreation areas* are intermediate both as to location and as to natural character. Such areas must ordinarily lie within one or two hours' travel time of most users; within this distance zone, the most attractive natural sites are, or should be, chosen. Most such areas are visited on a day-use basis. Many state parks fall in this category; so do most of the federal reservoir areas. Areas that provide opportunities for water skiing, skin diving, and power boating, as well as for swimming and fishing and picnicking, have become increasingly popular.

On each of these three major kinds of areas, use is much heavier at certain times than at others. Peak use tends to occur at certain hours each day on user areas, on certain days of the week at intermediate areas, and at certain seasons of the year at resource-based areas. If average use is very much lower than peak use, the cost per unit of use will be high if an effort is made to provide capacity to accommodate peak demand. A major economic problem of outdoor recreation, and indeed of all seasonal travel activities, is this irregularity and peaking of use.

Problems of increasing area to meet future needs differ for the three major kinds of recreation area. User-oriented areas must be provided as the cities grow; their problems are closely bound up with the city problems. Ample physical areas exist;

the difficult problems are their reservation at the critical time in city growth.

Resource-based areas are, by definition, unique areas, and their supply is strictly limited. We could not create another Grand Canyon or Yellowstone Park, no matter how we might try or how much we might spend. A few such additional areas might be set aside for public use, but total expansion possibilities are not large compared to the probable increases in demand.

The greatest possibilities for expansion lie with the intermediate areas. While scenically attractive areas are desirable, some quite nice parks can be developed from rather typical rural areas. A piece of rolling countryside with a small stream valley can be dammed to make an artificial lake with fixed overflow and constant shore line. Natural or planted woods surrounding the lake provide a place for camping, picnicking, hiking, horseback riding, nature study, and the like. The water body permits water-based sports. A number of state parks have been developed in this way.

A third way of classifying outdoor recreation areas is by ownership. A prime division is between publicly and privately owned. The public areas can be further subdivided according to the unit of government that provides them—federal, state, county, metropolitan agency, or city. At some levels of government, there are in turn different agencies, each with its particular kinds of areas and its separate legal authorization. Among the privately owned areas, some are used primarily or exclusively by the owner—the summer cottage, for example. Sometimes such facilities are rented to others, especially at seasons or times when the owner does not wish to use them. And there are other facilities catering to a paying public—resorts, lodges, fishing and hunting camps, and many others.

There is a substantial interrelationship between the physical or management classification of ORRRC, my economic classification, and any classification based on ownership of the facilities. This is suggested in table 3. A city park is a Class I high-density area, a user-oriented area, and city-owned; a national park is likely to be a Class IV unique natural area, a resource-based area, and federally owned, to use but two examples.

The various units of a system—however the latter may be structured or divided—are both complementary to each other and, to a degree, in competition with each other. Many people will use a city park (a user-oriented area) on weekdays throughout much of the year, a general outdoor recreation area in a state park (an intermediate area) on weekends, and a unique natural area in a national park (a resource-based area) during their vacation. For many people, enjoyment of one area appears to stimulate the use of other areas. The demands for the various kinds of areas are interconnected; a new park quickly attracts a volume of use, some of which is diverted from existing parks as well as some that is probably a net addition; or a new addition to population in any area throws new demands on existing parks, which may lead to a readjustment in their use as some become crowded. A park system is something like an electric power system, with load centers (cities and suburbs), generating facilities (parks), and transmission lines (highways); just as a new generator or a new load center forces a new operating procedure on all the old generators, a new unit in a park system brings new patterns of use to existing areas. In both planning and operating parks, this system aspect is a major factor to be considered; one can neither plan a park nor operate it as if it existed in isolation.

## Trends in Outdoor Recreation Activity and Area

Information about outdoor recreation activity on private land and at water areas tends to be general not statistical; and data are not available, or not available for a period of years, for some of the public areas. However, some of the foregoing discussion can be translated into statistics on area and number of visits.

Every available statistical measure shows that city and county parks are increasing in area, in intensity of management, and in use. The measures shown in figure 8—numbers of recreation leaders, numbers of supervised playgrounds, and numbers of recreation buildings and indoor centers—each show a rising trend over the past 50 or 60 years that is much steeper than the upward trend in urban population. The acreage of city parks

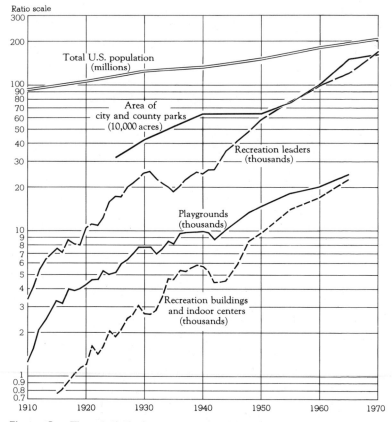

Figure 8.  The statistical measures in this chart show that city and county parks are increasing in area, in intensity of management, and in use. For particular cities, or certain areas of cities, however, parks may not be as "adequate" as the area figures suggest.

has trended upward about as fast as the population has increased. Some city parks have doubtless grown more crowded because many cities have increased their park acreage by adding large new parks on the outskirts. However, as the American people have generally grown more prosperous, they have increasingly turned to more distant recreation areas, and the increase in use of city parks has been less than it otherwise would have been.

The city parks are inadequate, in most cities, by standards of "adequacy" often used by park specialists. The latter is admittedly hard to define; location, accessibility, and improvements are as important as area. In any case, adequacy of parks is a little like adequacy of one's home—what can you afford? But there is little doubt that city parks, in nearly all cities, are least adequate in the very parts of the city that need them most— the lower-income sections, the ghettos, those occupied by racial and ethnic minorities. These sections of many cities were originally built at a time when provision for parks was less common, and parks can be added only with difficulty and at high cost. In many fairly large low-income sections of some cities, there is no park nor playground within walking distance. Children use the streets as a play area, but both they and adults lack satisfactory outdoor recreation areas with usable distances. If we really are concerned that poor people have access to parks, here is the place to spend our money and our effort.

Although some states have had parks for many years, the state park movement got a major impetus during the New Deal years of the 1930s, when various programs provided jobs for unemployed citizens who were then used to improve parks and build structures in them (figure 9). Today, every state has a park system, although some states have, many more parks, larger ones, and more heavily used ones than do other states. The acreage in all state parks has increased slowly for 30 years, and this in spite of several states having passed major bond issues for their parks. In general, states have chosen to spend a major part of their available capital funds in improving existing parks, rather than on buying additional land. This choice leads to more capacity to care for crowds in the short-run and for limited capital outlays, but it may be storing up trouble for a future day when existing areas are all used to capacity.

Especially noteworthy is the upward trend in attendance. This trend, while somewhat irregular, averages about 10 percent annually—several times the rate of increase in total population or in park acreage. The significant aspects of the trend are not only its steepness, but its persistence, with no clear evidence of a slowing down, and the fact that it is approximately constant

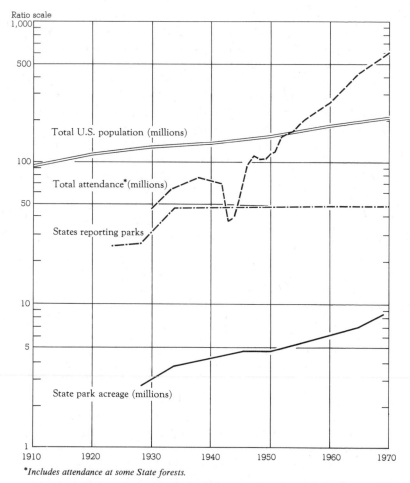

Ratio scale

*Includes attendance at some State forests.

**Figure 9.** On the whole, the states have chosen to spend their money on improving the capacity of existing parks rather than on acquiring more land, and the increase in attendance has far outpaced the increase in acreage at state parks.

on a percentage or ratio basis. Since the same general statements apply to some of the areas examined later, a further word about this type of trend is necessary. The fact that the percentage increase remains constant while total usage is increasing means that the actual number of visits is rising rapidly as their total number increases; the more outdoor recreation a population has, the more it wants, it seems. For instance, in the early 1950s the increase in recreation visits on national forests, from one year to the next, was 3 to 5 million visits; by the early 1960s the same percentage increase meant an actual increase of 10 to 15 million visits. An upward trend at a constant percentage rate results in ridiculous figures after a while, as anyone who has any experience whatever with a compound interest curve or other exponential rate realizes. Examples of these absurdities are cited later. But it is also noteworthy that figure 9 shows no sign of a slackening in rate of attendance growth as yet.

Well over 90 percent of all visits to state parks are day visits; overnight visits are only a small fraction of the total. For the most part, the state parks are intermediate areas in my system of classification.

On the whole, the federal reservoir areas are also intermediate areas. The Tennessee Valley Authority (TVA) reservoirs have long been popular recreation areas, but the area of the reservoirs has not been increasing rapidly in recent years and apparently attendance has hit something of a peak. In contrast, the Corps of Engineers is building many new reservoirs, with an increased area of water and of land committed to recreation, and attendance at such areas has increased very rapidly indeed (figure 10). The rate of increase in attendance slowed down somewhat in the early 1960s and then increased sharply in the later years, but growth throughout the decade did not match the explosive rate of the 1950s. Had the 1950s' rate continued until 2000, in that year every man, woman, and child in the United States would have had to spend 2,500 days a year at a corps reservoir—rather a difficult trick. This is the most dramatic example of what a constantly rising percentage growth leads to.

These reservoirs, and others built by or under the auspices of the Soil Conservation Service, have brought water bodies to regions of the country naturally lacking water bodies. At the same time, a technological revolution in water sports has been taking place—cheaper, better, and more mobile boats, with trailers; more powerful motors, at not correspondingly higher

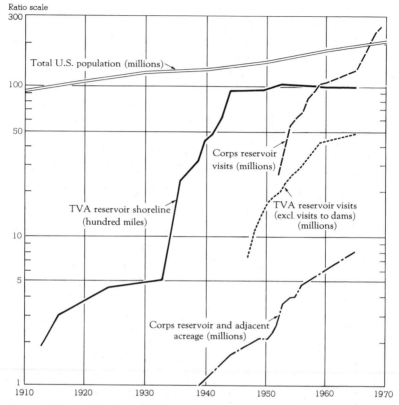

Figure 10. Increases in TVA reservoir areas and visits to these areas have been leveling off in recent years, but the Corps of Engineers has been building new reservoirs with land and water available for recreation purposes. As a result, visits to the Corps reservoirs have been increasing very rapidly.

costs, that could pull a boat fast enough for water skiing; water skis, scuba diving, and many other kinds of equipment. Thus, not only have the national trends in recreational use of water bodies been upward, but such use has become more common throughout the entire country.

Total recreation visits to the national park system and to national forests have increased steadily over the years, at an almost constant rate (figure 11). Particularly impressive is the

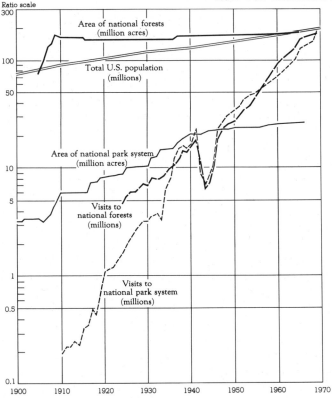

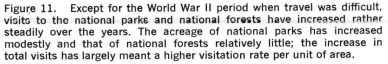

Figure 11. Except for the World War II period when travel was difficult, visits to the national parks and national forests have increased rather steadily over the years. The acreage of national parks has increased modestly and that of national forests relatively little; the increase in total visits has largely meant a higher visitation rate per unit of area.

long record for the national park system; since 1910, when total attendance was only 200,000, the rate has been almost steadily upward with attendance reaching over 172 million in 1970. The national park system has increased substantially during these decades, both in number of units and in total acreage, and it may be argued that this is a major reason for some of the increased attendance. However, attendance has risen at the same rate in the past 30 years when acreage was expanding slowly as it did earlier when the acreage was expanding faster, and an examination of the trend for parks of different ages (not shown in figure 11) reveals that the trend continues upward about as fast in the older as in the younger parks. Even more noteworthy is the experience of the national forests; although there have been some adjustments in boundaries, total acreage has remained almost constant for about 35 years while recreation attendance has mounted steadily and slightly more rapidly than attendance at the national park system.

The sharp dip in attendance at each type of area in the 1940s is significant. This was during World War II; tires and gasoline were rationed, and there was considerable social pressure exerted on workers to stay on the job rather than to take vacations. Personal incomes were high, but the other necessary factors for attendance at these resource-based areas were lacking. As a result, total attendance fell off by two-thirds. It recovered very rapidly when the war was over, but only to the prewar level, not to the prewar trend line; as far as attendance was concerned, the war was simply a period of hibernation. The wartime decline and postwar recovery is one of the most dramatic and best illustrations of the role transportation plays in outdoor recreation.

The trend in attendance at each of these types of federal areas has ranged between 8 percent and 10 percent annually. The previous comments about exponential trends apply here also. Attendance cannot increase at this rate forever, but there is no clear evidence of a slackening off yet. Since most of the visits to the federal areas are made on weekends or during vacations, trends in the amount of leisure available at these times, especially for vacations, will have a major effect upon recreation use of these areas.

With the possible exception of the city parks (where data on attendance are the weakest), the rate of growth in attendance at major kinds of public outdoor recreation areas has been about 8 to 10 percent annually. Since population, leisure, income per capita, and travel were increasing at a lower rate—about 2 percent annually—the increase in recreation attendance seems to be attributable to a combination of these factors rather than to any one alone. That is, more people without higher average incomes, better transportation, and more leisure would have resulted in much less growth in outdoor recreation; or higher real incomes per capita without more leisure and better transportation would have also resulted in lower attendance; and so on. This view gains considerably from the wartime experience when transportation was restricted.

## PRESERVATION OF QUALITY IN OUTDOOR RECREATION

The steady and rapid rise in numbers of visitors to many outdoor recreation areas has raised serious problems for the maintenance of the quality of the areas concerned. Too many people can have serious physical impact on an area—the human foot can be as destructive as the bulldozer, if there are too many feet. More seriously, those psychological aspects of the scene which were its initial attraction may be lost; surely this is the case for those who seek solitude and Nature, but too many fishermen may spoil the area for fishermen also. There is grave danger that preoccupation with rising numbers of visitors will obscure what is happening to the quality of the area and of the recreation experience.

What can be done to preserve the quality of the recreation experience? First of all, visitors need some education, at home or at the site, about the consequences of careless or willful acts; if everyone left just one piece of facial tissue or discarded one cigarette pack, the whole place would soon be knee-deep in them. Educational programs for control of litter, such as Keep America Beautiful and other organizations have put on, can be helpful here. A few visitors may have to be disciplined, when their acts are willful rather than careless. Most states now have fines for littering highways; they may have fewer fines for littering their parks or less obvious signs, or they may not be enforcing their anti-littering ordinances effectively.

Parks and other outdoor recreation areas must be well maintained if the quality of the recreation experience is not to deteriorate. If the area is clean, and if garbage cans or trash barrels are conveniently located and regularly emptied, visitors will be more likely to deposit their litter in the designated receptacles than they will if these conditions are not met. My sons and I once stopped for lunch at a highway wayside in a midwestern state, where the ground was covered by newspapers dated more than two years earlier, and by garbage and trash of an apparently similar age. Such conditions do not encourage one to be scrupulous in disposing of litter and garbage.

Recreation areas must be physically maintained in other ways also. Improvements must be kept up, and sanitary facilities kept clean. If trees, shrubs, or grass begin to show severe signs of wear, they must be restored in some way, or usage reduced in some way. In a great many parks where camping is encouraged, there are signs warning against cutting trees and shrubs, yet there is no wood supply or not a convenient one available for the campfire that many visitors regard as one of the necessary aspects of camping; the managers of such parks are, in effect, inviting visitors to disobey the rules.

There is some capacity beyond which use of any recreation area cannot increase without serious physical consequences. Resource managers long ago learned that there is a maximum sustained yield rate of forage harvest from grazing lands or of timber harvest from forest lands, and this same concept applies to recreation lands as well. When the potential demand exceeds the carrying capacity of a recreation area, there are several steps that can be taken to bring them into balance. First of all, recreation areas should be acquired and developed elsewhere to provide additional opportunities for recreationists. It may also be necessary to place some kind of ceiling on attendance at an area; this could be enforced by requiring advance reservations and admitting people without reservation only when there was unused capacity, or by requiring people to line up and wait their turn, or by setting prices that discourage the more casual visitors, or by other devices or by combinations of these. Where demand is excessive, the alternative to the foregoing measures is deterioration of the area; in time its value will sink so low that few people will want to visit them.

Wilderness areas, some historical areas, and some other recreation areas are particularly likely to suffer physical destruction and loss of psychological value, if use is unrestricted. In many historical areas, the number of visitors is now limited in some way; visitors are sometimes conducted in groups (as in the White House), or they may have to line up to file past some spot or display. The necessity for such action is easily seen under these circumstances, but so far no one has faced up to the need for limiting visits to wilderness areas, whose value is destroyed by noise and crowds.

One means of preserving the quality of the recreation experience is to limit activities to those for which the area is best suited and to divert other activities to other suitable areas. In resource management, it is always wasteful to use scarce and valuable resources for purposes for which more common and less valuable resources would do equally well. It is no more foolish to specify clear lumber when common would do, or to use stainless steel when ordinary steel would do equally well, than it is to permit motorboating and water skiing in wilderness areas, especially if enough motorboating and skiing waters are available elsewhere.

Problems of maintenance of quality of the outdoor recreation experience are not limited to public areas. The operator of a private campground is under considerable temptation to squeeze in a few more campsites and to admit a few more campers, for often his profits seem to lie in a little larger volume of business; his costs do not rise as fast as his income, when intensity of use rises. Or he may be tempted to erect advertising signs to draw in larger numbers of visitors even though these signs disfigure his landscape. In each case, he may achieve a short-run monetary gain at the expense of a long-run loss in quality. Pressure to meet his competition may also lead him to manage his recreation resource in ways that he would otherwise not choose.

The problem of maintaining the quality of the recreation experience is not unlike the problem of soil conservation on farmland, or the problem of maintaining neighborhood quality in a residential area. In each case, there is the problem of building or preserving for the future, as well as the problem of living in the present. There are no painless answers; even drifting may well lead to undesirable results, if not disaster.

VALUE OF NATURAL RESOURCES USED
FOR OUTDOOR RECREATION

The rising demand for outdoor recreation and the frequent competition between outdoor recreation and other uses of land and water resources have focused attention on the value of such resources when used for outdoor recreation. Private property of this kind has a price, as anyone who has tried to buy a site at a lake or in the mountains quickly learns, but there is no market price to measure the value of public outdoor recreation areas. Public recreation areas are often available to users without charge or at more or less arbitrary charges that do not reflect the full value of the site, and prices charged by private developers of outdoor recreation areas are, to some extent, limited by the low charges on public areas. A private campground operator, for example, cannot charge much more for camping on his area than the public park down the road charges; a higher charge is likely to be sustained by reason of his superior services and does not measure a return to his resource per se. Since the market in outdoor recreation is far from being fully competitive, one must devise other measures for the value of outdoor recreation.

Whenever it is necessary to develop estimates of the value of goods or services not sold competitively, the results may be far better than no estimates but they still remain estimates, not competitive prices. In the case of outdoor recreation, the best approach is through economic analysis of the whole outdoor recreation experience, which includes expenditures made at home, enroute to and from the site, and at the site itself. Expenses at the site may or may not include an entrance or a user fee or a service charge such as a boat launching charge. Presumably every outdoor recreationist goes as often as he can afford, given his tastes, his income, his leisure, and his location with respect to the recreation area. When visits are expressed in terms of number of visits per thousand of base population, there are more visits from the nearby areas than from the more distant areas (see table 4). In this hypothetical example, rate of attendance falls off rapidly with increased cost (cost including travel as well as any user charge at the site). In practice, use may decline rapidly for sites

TABLE 4. DEMAND SCHEDULE OF WHOLE EXPERIENCE
FOR HYPOTHETICAL RECREATION AREA

| Zone | Population | Cost per visit | Number of visits | Visits per 1,000 base population |
|------|-----------|----------------|------------------|----------------------------------|
| 1 | 1,000 | $1 | 500 | 500 |
| 2 | 4,000 | $3 | 1,200 | 300 |
| 3 | 10,000 | $5 | 1,000 | 100 |

with weak drawing power or slowly for sites with strong drawing power, but a relationship between distance and decay is universal.

Table 4 shows only the demand for the whole recreation experience. To get a demand for the resources of the site, further calculations are necessary. Assuming that all large groups of users react in the same way to an increase in costs, it is possible to estimate the number of visitors if the entrance fee or other user charge is raised by specified amounts (table 5). In this hypothetical case, there would be 2,700 visitors if there were no charge for using the area; 1,200 if the charge were $1; 700 if the charge were $2; and so on. As a matter of fact, these estimates might understate use at the higher charges because they reflect added monetary costs only—the time cost of travel would not be increased. In this simple example, the largest revenue would be obtained at a charge of $2; beyond this point the increase in

TABLE 5. EFFECT OF INCREASES IN THE ATTENDANCE FEE ON
NUMBERS OF VISITS TO HYPOTHETICAL RECREATION AREA

| Zone | Number of visits at added cost[1] per visit of | | | | | |
|------|------|------|------|------|------|------|
| | No charge | $1 | $2 | $3 | $4 | $5 |
| 1 | 500 | 400 | 300 | 200 | 100 | 0 |
| 2 | 1,200 | 800 | 400 | 0 | 0 | 0 |
| 3 | 1,000 | 0 | 0 | 0 | 0 | 0 |
| Total attendance | 2,700 | 1,200 | 700 | 200 | 100 | 0 |
| Total receipts | 0 | $1,200 | $1,400 | $600 | $400 | 0 |

[1] In addition to regular travel cost.

receipts from higher charges would be offset by the decrease in number of visitors. Were charges to be varied by a dime or a nickel, the exact point might not be $2 but some other figure between $1 and $3.

The foregoing assumes that a single price is charged for entrance to the recreation area. Suppose, instead, that all persons who would pay $3 or more were charged $3, that all persons who would pay $2 or more but not as much as $3 were charged $2, that all persons who would pay $1 or more but not as much as $2 were charged $1; the total revenue that could be collected would then be higher than at any single fee—in this case, about $2,200 in total, compared with $1,400 at a single fee of $2. It probably would be impractical to impose any such discriminatory pricing system, but it does illustrate the nature of the demand. If every user could be charged every cent he would pay to use the area, the total sum would be still higher. This type of charge system does not lend itself to practical application, but it may be argued that the total arrived at in this way is a measure of the total benefit to society because it is the sum of the maximum value of the site to each user.

Whether one chooses to use the single charge that produces the maximum revenue or whether one chooses to use the maximum sum derived from each individual's maximum value, the amounts estimated for outdoor recreation will be comparable with estimated values from electric power generation, irrigation, forestry, or any other use of the same land and water so long as all the uses are estimated in the same way. In each case, for projects proposed but not in operation, the results will be no more than estimates of future relationships, which may or may not prove to be accurate.

This procedure measures the economic benefits from outdoor recreation that show up in visits to the area. In some lake or reservoir areas there is private property whose use does not show up in the statistics on attendance at the public areas, but whose value has been increased by the construction of the reservoir or by the management of the lake. In such cases, it is perfectly proper to add this increment in the value of private property to the value created at the public recreation site to get a total value of the resource for outdoor recreation.

There may also be substantial economic impact upon the local area, from provision of goods and services to recreation visitors. Part of their total expenditures are for services performed or value added locally, but part are for goods and services "imported" into the local area from elsewhere. The value added by services to outside visitors is expressed in wages and profits locally, and this in turn produces a demand for more goods and local services—a multiplier effect. The total impact of the recreation or tourist trade may be considerable; in fact, it is the prime economic support for many areas in the United States and in other countries. The gain from a particular recreation site is often local rather than national, however. The economic impact is likely to be felt by the area where the site is located and along the main routes to that area; the nation as a whole would probably gain as much from an equivalent site located elsewhere. Outdoor recreation in total surely has an economic impact upon the national economy, particularly upon those activities which produce goods and services directly used in outdoor recreation.

## Who Pays, and How?

The great increase in outdoor recreation and the consequent need for land and water areas exclusively or largely devoted to this use raise important questions about how the costs are to be paid. There is a considerable tradition of "free" public parks in the United States. There are several defenses for government (at some level) providing parks for public use: the area may have unique resource or cultural values that would be lost or jeopardized in private ownership; there may be important social benefits from park availability (decreased juvenile delinquency, etc.) ; the scale at which the park must be reserved and provided may be greater, for some years, than the most profitable scale; and others. The idea of "free" parks is justified on the grounds that they are most beneficial, socially, to the groups that cannot afford to pay for them.

Actually, of course, the whole outdoor recreation experience is rarely free; even when no entrance or use charge is made, the visitor has to bear the costs of getting to the area. And every public outdoor recreation area entails costs that are borne by the public. The question of how these costs should be met raises issues of equity or fairness, of efficiency in park use and management, and of practical politics.

There are several broad alternative ways of financing the costs of public parks. Their costs may be paid out of the general revenues of the unit of government providing the park, in which case those who pay the taxes are the ones who pay for the parks. Or their costs may be paid by some special tax; some states have levied a cigarette tax to finance state parks, apparently because this type of tax is easy to collect and raises a considerable sum of money and not because cigarette smokers gain unusual benefits from state parks. Or the capital costs of acquiring and developing a park may be borne by a bond issue. This does not really settle the issue of who pays; it merely postpones it. Or part of all the costs may be met by some form of user charges—entrance fees to the park, parking fees in the park, charges for special services such as boat launching, camping fees, and the like. In this case, the users pay the costs. There seems a certain equity in this; many taxpayers use the public parks rarely if at all, and receive little benefit from their availability. Entrance fees do add to user costs, but most people who can afford to own an auto and pay the other costs of visiting parks can bear modest user charges as well. For the large numbers of truly poor people, user charges mean little; they cannot afford to go to the park in any case, and the total taxes they pay may be affected little by park expenditures.

User charges might also be used as a tool in park management. Imposing charges for only some days of the week or some seasons might shift some of the use; and charging more at one area than at another might shift some use toward a lightly used area. Charges might also cause people to value the recreation experience more highly and to take better care of the area. User charges should not be imposed in areas or under circumstances when it would be excessively costly to collect them or when their collection could readily be evaded. The purpose and the rationale of any charges should be explained carefully to users in order to reduce public resistance to them to a minimum. A decade or more ago, many park administrators were afraid the public would rebel at user charges; experience with both public and private areas shows that most recreationists are quite willing to pay their share of costs, and resistance to paying has been limited.

# CHAPTER FIVE

# *Cropland*

Farming in the United States today is a business—a way of organizing land, labor, production materials, and management capability to produce a salable output of agricultural commodities. The commercial farmer buys machinery, fertilizer, feed, chemicals, and other productive inputs and sells all or virtually all of his output on the market. For the whole of American agriculture, the cost of purchased inputs is about 70 percent of the value of the output; the value added on the farm is only about 30 percent.

In an earlier day in the United States, as in most of the world today, farming was a way of life rather than a business. Farmers worked in traditional ways, buying few inputs, consuming most of their own output, selling relatively little. They followed agriculture as a way of life because they had grown up on the farm and because farming was all they knew. Although that kind of farming has largely gone from the United States, there are still several hundred thousand small farmers who stay in farming because they do not know what else they might do for a living; their inputs and outputs and incomes are all very low.

Our information about land use in farming is some of the best for any land use. A census of agriculture has been taken for 100 years or more, in varying but generally increasing detail; for more than 40 years it has been taken at five-year intervals. The census uses land use and other definitions that have been tested many times, and its coverage of farms is nearly, if not wholly complete.

Not all of the land in "farms," as defined by the census, is used for cropland. Some is used for forestry and some for raising cattle, sheep, and goats. These uses are discussed later—grazing land in chapter 6, and forests in chapter 7.

Certain physical characteristics make land suitable for crops; deep, well-drained, medium-textured, level or gently sloping soils, and favorable climatic conditions are particularly advantageous features. But the whole concept of cropland is partly an economic one. It is easier to grow crops on good cropland than on poor cropland, and to grow them where there is good transportation to markets, but it is possible to grow crops under some quite unfavorable conditions. Indeed, for the world as a whole, large acreages of crops are grown on lands that American farmers would not consider as suitable cropland. Through a long process of trial and error, American farmers have sorted out the land that they think is best suited for crops, and millions of acres of land that were once used for crops, particularly in hill country for a subsistence type of agriculture, are no longer used for this purpose. We are generously endowed with cropland in the United States; about 300 million acres of land are now used for crop production, and another 300 million acres could be shifted to the growing of crops if the need were urgent. The sorting of land into that best suited for crops and that less suited for them is much influenced by the prevailing technology of agricultural production. As technology changes, some land becomes desirable that previously was less so; and the sorting out process is never completed.

PRESENT CROPLAND USE

Although almost every county in the United States has some land that is used for crops (figure 12), the great areas of cropland are in the Middle West where gentle topography, medium-textured, deep soils, adequate but not excessive natural moisture and internal drainage, and good native fertility make the land suitable for crop production. Modest deficiencies in one or more of these physical characteristics are not too serious, but larger deficiencies make crop production increasingly difficult. Modern technology enables farmers to overcome some deficiencies. Irrigation may supply water where natural sources are too limited, or drainage and flood protection may remove excess natural water supplies, or fertilizers may offset deficiencies in natural fertility,

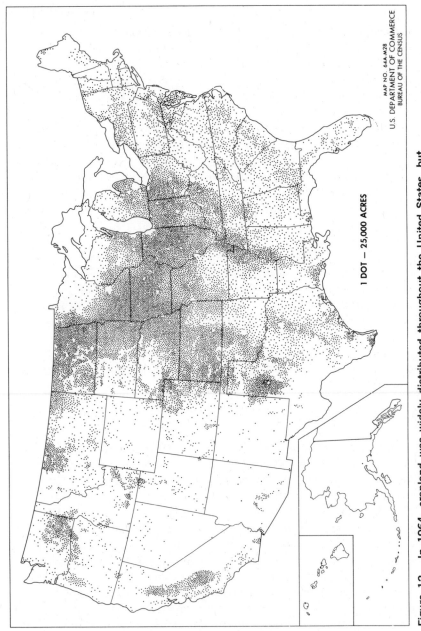

1 DOT = 25,000 ACRES

MAP NO. 64A-M28
U.S. DEPARTMENT OF COMMERCE
BUREAU OF THE CENSUS

Figure 12. In 1964, cropland was widely distributed throughout the United States, but the great concentrations were—and still are—in the Midwest.

but most of these measures impose additional costs. The fact that natural soils or soils modified by various actions can be used to produce good crops does not always mean that it is profitable to do so. The land may earn more in another use; there may be so much good land that its full output would depress farm commodity prices to unprofitable levels; or transportation to market may be too costly. These or any one of several other reasons may limit the use of physically suitable land. In the competitive agricultural world of today, the "lay of the land," or the ability to organize farming into large fields in which large machinery can be used effectively, is one very important factor. The cropland pattern shown in figure 12 represents the decisions of more than 3 million farmers in 1964 about the land best suited for crop production and is the product of the trial and error process of land selection mentioned above. (More recent data were not available when this book was written; publication of the 1969 Census of Agriculture is scheduled for late 1971.)

There have been some substantial changes in cropland use within the past two decades (table 6). In the early postwar years (represented in the table by 1950), total "cropland" was 478 acres, of which some was idle (mostly under government acreage retirement programs) and a good deal was used only for pasture. Of the acreage actually used for crops, about two-thirds was used to produce hay and grain for livestock and nearly a fourth to produce grain for human consumption. The great cash crops, such as cotton, soybeans, fruits and vegetables, and tobacco, required only about 15 percent of the total crop acreage—they accounted for a much higher percentage of the value of farm crops, however, and used more labor. This early postwar period was one of high demand for agricultural commodities, domestically and for export; there were few governmental limitations on cropland use. Reasonably full use was made of the land then usable for crops on existing farms; a great deal more land could have been cleared of forests, or drained, or irrigated if the long-term demand prospects warranted.

By the late 1960s, the acreage actually used for crops had declined by about 50 million acres. Acreage declines were evident in each major crop group except oil crops, where the great in-

TABLE 6.  MAJOR USE OF CROPLAND

(*million acres*)

| Kind of use | 1950 | 1964 |
|---|---|---|
| Cropland used only for pasture | 69 | 57 |
| Cropland idle or in cover crops | 22 | 52 |
| Cropland used for crops, including cultivated fallow | 387 | 335 |
| Total | 478 | 444 |
| | 1949–51 average | 1966–68 average |
| Cropland harvested | 345 | 296 |
| Planted crop acreage[1] | | |
| Feed grains | 147 | 114 |
| Food grains | 82 | 62 |
| Hay and forage | 79 | 69 |
| Oil crops | 19 | 41 |
| Cotton | 24 | 10 |
| Vegetables and potatoes | 5 | 5 |
| Fruits and nuts | 3 | 3 |
| Tobacco | 2 | 1 |
| Sugar crops | 1 | 2 |

*Sources:* Data for 1950 and 1964 are from U.S. Department of Commerce, *Census of Agriculture, 1964*. Data for 1949–51 and 1966–68 are from U.S. Department of Agriculture, *Agricultural Statistics*, annual.

*Note:* 1964 data are used because the 1969 Census of Agriculture was not published when this table was prepared in the spring of 1971.

[1] Where data permitted, planted acreage; otherwise, harvested acreage.

creases in soybean acreage resulted in an overall increase. Much less land was used for feed grains, food grains, hay and forage, and cotton, and there were either smaller reductions or no increase for tobacco, fruits, and vegetables. All of these changes in acreage occurred at a time when agricultural output was increasing rather steadily, at an average rate of 2 percent or more per year. About half of the approximately 50 million acres that went out of crop production moved into other uses. The other half continued to be classed as cropland but was left idle or used for cover crops; this was due in large part to expanded federal programs for crop acreage reduction, such as the Soil Bank and its successors. Thus, in spite of increasing population and increasing total demand for agricultural commodities, the acreage used for crops declined by about 15 percent over this period. The acreage of crops will probably not increase much, if any, for another generation; there will be some modest additions here and there, and some modest retirements or losses elsewhere, but the present acreage of cropland should be able to produce all the agricultural commodities for which there will be an effective demand.

## POTENTIAL CROPLAND AND POTENTIAL AGRICULTURAL OUTPUT

The United States has a large supply of land that could be farmed permanently but is not used for this purpose. Potential cropland, like cropland proper, has a physical and an economic dimension, and land that would have to be abandoned after producing crops for only a few years should not be considered cropland.

The Soil Conservation Service has developed a land capability classification that includes slope, soil type, past and potential erosion hazard, and other factors. Class I soils are the best, requiring no special measures of soil management beyond those required to maintain their fertility; Class II soils require modest conservation practices to offset their modest limitations for crop production; Class III soils require more intensive conservation practices to offset their greater limitations, and may be used less intensively and often for a narrower range of crops. Class IV soils have severe limitations for crop production, and require careful management to avoid severe erosion; by and large, this class of soils is marginal for crop production, although some areas are well-suited for specialty crops, such as fruit trees. Classes V, VI, and VII include soils that are considered unsuitable for crop production under most conditions; if used, they require very special measures for their protection and their uses are limited to a narrow range of crops.

In 1967, when a comprehensive inventory of land uses in relation to land characteristics was undertaken, about three-fourths of the Class I land, about 60 percent of the Class II land, and nearly half of the Class III land was actually used for crops (figure 13); most of the other land in these three classes was in forest and woodland or in pasture and range, with about equal areas in each. It is also noteworthy that about a fourth of the Class IV land, about 6 percent of the Class V land, and smaller fractions of land in Classes VI, VII, and VIII were also used for crops. These data suggest that there is some correlation—but not a close one—between land capability as the soils specialists rated it, and cropland as carried out by farmers. However, it should be pointed out that even if each farmer were to use his best land for crops, American farmers as a whole

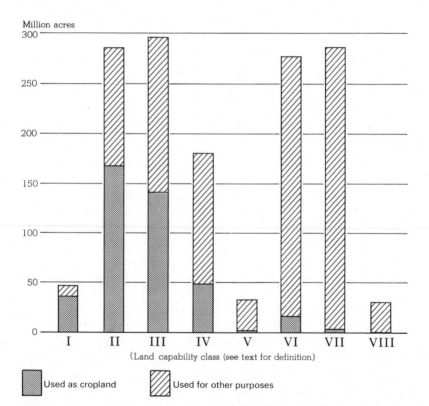

Figure 13. A high percentage of the land in the top three soil categories is used as cropland; most of the other land in these classes is in forest or woodland or in pasture or range. The reasons for some of the land with poorer soils being used for cropland are discussed in the text.

might not be using the best land in the nation for crops. Each farmer is limited to the land within his own farm. If his capacity to farm exceeds his acreage of good cropland, he may use some of his poorer land for crops; if his area of good cropland exceeds his capacity to farm, he will have good cropland not in crops. Thus, some discrepancy between land capability classification and land use is inevitable.

There are other reasons why some of the better land is not used for crops. In some cases, farmers may simply not know its capabilities because they have not tried to use it for crops. More commonly, some expenditures would be required to bring the land into cropping condition; trees would have to be cleared, stones removed, drains installed, or special soil conservation or other measures undertaken. The individual farmer might find it worthwhile to clear a patch of woods on good land to increase his cropped acreage. But in many cases the cost of bringing the land into production would exceed the gains that could be secured from its use. Nevertheless, this land capable of cropping but not now used for this purpose represents a large reservoir of potential cropland; the acreage in the first three land classes is almost equal to the total acreage of harvested crops today.

Instead of dipping into this reservoir, American agriculture has used other means to expand its output to meet the increased demand for its products. Increases in output have come from higher crop yields and larger outputs from livestock. Crop varieties have been improved, more fertilizer has been used, chemicals have been used to control weeds and insects, larger machinery has been brought into use. The combined effect of these and other measures has been an intensification of agriculture on a relatively limited acreage. However, the adoption and use of such measures has been inhibited by the unfavorable price-cost relationships that have faced farmers in recent years.

Despite its output, American agriculture has rarely produced at its full capacity. Throughout our history, it has been the demand for agricultural commodities that has very largely governed their supply. Had the markets been available at profitable prices, our farmers could have quickly increased their output. In time of war or of booming prosperity, they materially stepped up agricultural output, often in spite of shortages of materials and labor.

At present, and for the next decade or two at least, American agriculture has a large unused productive potential. If prices were more favorable than at present, and seemed likely to remain so, and if markets would absorb everything that could be produced, farmers could materially step up their output—a 50 percent increase in 10 years is wholly possible. This estimate does not depend upon any new and striking technological change, but rather upon fuller use of presently known means of production.

Under something like present agricultural prices and government programs, the agricultural surplus seems to be a permanent fixture of the American scene. Nonfarmers often do not realize the built-in mechanisms leading to constantly larger farm output. A large government research organization constantly provides new information; so do the private firms supplying fertilizer, seed, feed, chemicals, machinery, and other production materials for farmers. The farmer who can find a way of increasing his output, from his own labor and land, will almost always find it to his advantage to do so. He gains, even though the total effect of all farmers so reacting may be an increased output that lowers prices enough to reduce gross agricultural income. An individual farmer cannot afford to neglect any opportunities for increased output at lower cost per unit. Many of his costs are overhead—his own labor, to a large extent, and the costs of a minimum set of farm machinery. A greater output from the same land, labor, and machinery often means a greater income, at least until other farmers follow suit and prices drop accordingly.

There seems little reason for concern about the nation's ability to feed itself. By increasing agricultural output and by shifting to more cereals and less meat in the national diet, the country can feed 10, or 20, or even more *times* its present population, by the time population reaches such a level—if it ever does. The ultimate food productive capacity is so far above the present level that there is nothing to be gained from trying to estimate just how large it is. The problems of agriculture for our generation, and for the next one, lie in different directions. And the population problem is infinitely more complex than sheer ability to produce food.

## CROPLAND HEALTH

Americans, from the earliest colonial days onward, have been profligate in their use of land; at first, there was so much land, in relation to the need for it, that there was little incentive to protect and care for that in use. Some of the land that was cleared and used for crops in fairly early colonial days was abandoned a few decades later; the farmer or the planter moved to new land and cleared it. Much less was then known about soils and their management; most farmers would not have known how to control erosion or to maintain fertility, even if they had desired to do so. The strong individualism of the pioneer and the development of the extreme concept of fee simple ownership made land use very much an individual or personal matter. If a man chose to use his land in such a way that the topsoil ran off into the streams, silting them up, whose business was it, except his own?

Exploitation of cropland continued unabated, perhaps increased, as settlement spread across the country. Some lands were more easily eroded than others, and, in some areas, wind was more of a threat than water. In nearly all areas, soils when first cleared had fertility stored up through forest or prairie use over the preceding centuries, which was quickly used up by cropping. Protests against this exploitative use were voiced throughout the nineteenth century, and more and more concern was expressed in the twentieth century, but comparatively little was done to remedy the situation until the late 1920s. Research on erosion control began at that time, but only on a modest scale.

The 1930s brought widespread drought and wind erosion on a frightening scale; great storms carried dust from the Great Plains to the Atlantic Ocean where some was deposited on ships at sea. The magnitude and drama of these dust storms stirred many people, urban as well as rural, who had previously been uninformed or unconcerned about erosion. At the same time, several million workers were unemployed, and large-scale public works and relief projects were begun by the federal government. Many of these projects were concerned with natural resources in one way or another, and many were directed toward the problems of soil erosion.

About this time, a soils specialist, Hugh H. Bennett, became deeply disturbed about soil losses and began his crusade for soil conservation measures. Bennett was like a Biblical prophet, stirring people in part by the very intensity of his convictions. He aroused the public and channelled a general public concern about soil erosion into specific public and private actions. One of the major results of the soil conservation movement was the development of the soil conservation district, as a special unit of government, governed by elected committeemen (usually farmers) and working with public agencies and private individuals. Now, virtually all farmland in the United States is included in a soil conservation district.

When a federal survey of soil conservation was made in 1967, it was found that 36 percent of the cropland had either been "adequately treated" by that date or had never required special conservation treatment. Some lands were judged to require further treatment of one kind or another depending upon such factors as their location, climate, soil type, and slope, as well as on the degree and form of past erosion. It was also found that in some parts of the country where cropland had been severely eroded and taken out of crop production, largely for economic reasons, Nature had at least partially healed the scars resulting from earlier use. This was the case in the Piedmont areas of the Southeast, which had one of the worst soil erosion situations in the country in the mid-1930s. The combination of varied topography, steep slopes, erodable soils, and small fields devoted to row crops such as cotton led to sheet erosion and many gulleys. In the past 50 years, but especially since the mid-1930s, more than half of the former cropland has been abandoned. Weeds, shrubs, and ultimately trees grow up on the abandoned fields, and the soil erosion comes largely to a stop. In the Great Plains, erosion was reduced when some cropland went back into grass (or weeds) after the wheat reduction programs came into effect; some of this gain was lost in the World War II plow-up for increased wheat acreage, but there has been some comeback since then.

The health of American cropland is far better today than it was during the 1920s, largely as a result of public programs of technical assistance, education, and subsidy. But there are still millions of acres from which soil losses are relatively great, and the steady erosion not only downgrades the land but causes both immediate and long-term damage to streams and other water bodies. Wind also takes its toll, in some years. Unfortunately— and all too often—the cost of an adequate job of soil conservation is not offset by a corresponding increase in farm income. The need for both public and private action still continues.

## AN AGRICULTURAL REVOLUTION

The land use changes described in this chapter are but one aspect of the agricultural revolution that has been taking place over the past half century. During the nineteenth century and the early years of the twentieth century, when the tide of settlement was sweeping westward, there were increases in total farm population, in the number of acres of land in farms and the acreage in cultivation; and in the numbers of horses and mules —this being the era when motive power was literally horse power. This whole process reached a peak about the time of World War I (see figure 14). The first indication that such a peak had been reached was a leveling off in crop acreage and in numbers of horses and mules.

Farm population stayed on a broad undulating plateau from about 1910 to about 1940; farm-raised boys and girls migrated to the cities, but in numbers that left the farm population approximately constant. With the coming of World War II, farm population began a nose dive, which carried it from about 30 million people down to about 10 million today.

In the past 50 years there has been a virtually complete shift from animal to mechanical power on farms. Numbers of horses and mules declined from a peak of approximately 25 million to about 3 or 4 million. The U.S. Department of Agriculture no longer publishes figures on numbers of horses and mules, apparently because they are no longer important as draft animals. Those that are left are likely to be riding animals; the horse is still important on ranches. The sight of a team of horses pulling a plow or of a mule pulling a cultivator today would be nearly as much of a curiosity as a yoke of oxen doing the same tasks. Forty years ago, when I first began working professionally in agriculture, we wondered if the day would ever come when there would be any farm wholly without animal power; today there are a few million. Somewhat less than 5 million tractors now provide more horsepower than the somewhat more than 20 million horses and mules that they replaced. And trucks have taken over the job of hauling goods to and from farms.

This shift in source of power has been accompanied by a major reduction in human labor used in agriculture. Total man-hours used in agricultural production have declined to about a third of their peak, and are still declining. The decline in numbers of horses and mules seems to have stopped, and numbers may have stabilized at a low level; likewise, the increase in numbers (but not in horsepower) of tractors seems to

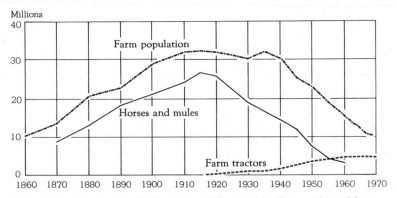

Figure 14. The decline in farm population and in the number of horses and mules and the increase in the number of farm tractors is one aspect of the agricultural revolution that has been taking place over the past half-century.

have come to an end. There are now about 1½ tractors per farm, on the average; some farms, such as specialized poultry plants, have none, and some farms have several. The number of farm people has not yet reached bottom; an equilibrium number is likely to be less than 5 million, compared with the 10 million there now.

The shifts in use of human and animal power and in cropland use are only part of the story. Agricultural output has risen rather steadily (except for downward dips during the years of severe drought in the 1930s) at a rate of about 2 percent annually (figure 15). It is this sharp contrast between rate of

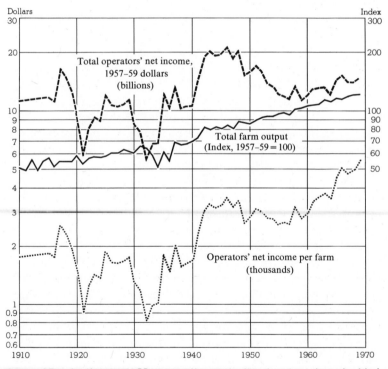

**Figure 15.** In the past 60 years, the agricultural output has doubled, while total net income to all farm operators has moved up and down but increased relatively little in real terms. For the past 30 years, net income per farm has risen, as the total number of farmers has shrunk.

labor and land input, on the one hand, and the total output, on the other, that justifies the term "revolution." The data do not tell the whole story. As noted earlier, there have been major changes in crop varieties, in use of fertilizers, in use of other chemicals such as pesticides and weedicides, and in technology generally. Many kinds of machines other than tractors have been involved also.

Changes in farm income are still another aspect of the agricultural revolution (figure 15). In real income terms (constant prices), agriculture as a whole gained relatively little between 1910 and 1969. There were sharp dips in the post-World War I depression and in the Great Depression of the 1930s, and there was a boom period during and after World War II, but agricultural income was not much higher in 1969 than it was in 1910, although agriculture was producing $2\frac{1}{2}$ times what it had produced 60 years earlier. The terms of trade moved against agriculture over this period, somewhat unevenly but with special rapidity from the mid-1940s to about 1960. American farmers were in somewhat the same situation as the producers of raw materials in the less-developed countries of the world, who also saw the terms of trade move against them in the same period. One may well argue that the 1940s and the early postwar years were abnormal, but to farmers the trends since then have been far from encouraging. There has been some modest improvement since 1960, but total net income in constant dollars has increased only about in proportion to increased farm output.

One of the most important and basic factors underlying this agricultural revolution has been the research and education of the U.S. Department of Agriculture and the agricultural colleges. New crop varieties, new methods of production, new chemicals, new machines, and other new productive inputs were developed and put into use by farmers. Private industry expanded to produce these inputs and to devise additional ones. A whole new technology of agricultural production evolved, was made available to farmers, and was put into use by them.

Two economic aspects of this transformation of agriculture deserve special note. First of all, the internal economics of the typical farm drove the farmer to adopt new methods if they were within his financial and personal capacity, even when the result to farmers as a group was no higher income. Many farm production costs are fixed, irrespective of output, and an increase in output often comes at a lower marginal cost than the average cost of production. Especially noteworthy in this respect is the cost of living (or of labor) of the farmer himself; the demands of his family for a modern living spur him on to produce as much income as he can, and make it impossible for him to cut back his output very much even when prices are unfavorable. At the same time, the output of each farmer is such a small fraction of the total production that his effect upon market prices is negligible. The typical farmer is driven to adopt new methods of production, which are nearly always output-increasing in their effect, even when his income, and the income of agriculture as a whole, is not increased thereby. He has to run fast not to lose his competitive position; the early successful adopters gain, the laggards lose.

The other economic aspect of the agricultural revolution stems from the increase in urban incomes. Farm youth are most unwilling to enter farming when income prospects are so much better in the cities. Nearly all of the reduction in numbers of farm people and in numbers of farms has been due to the unwillingness of young men to enter farming; very little has been due to an accelerated withdrawal of older farmers from farming.

Income to agriculture as a whole (in constant dollars) declined sharply from the late 1940s until the late 1950s and then more or less stabilized, whereas income per average farm declined only modestly in the earlier period and has risen considerably since the late 1950s. The divergence of these trends is due to the sharply declining numbers of farms; with only about half as many farms now as there were during the World War II period, the total income for agriculture is split among fewer farmers. By greatly increasing the size of their business, farmers have managed to increase their incomes (in constant dollars) slightly.

The pace of change has been swift, however, and some farmers have not been able to take advantage of it, in part because their assets (including landholdings) were too small or their personal capacities too limited or both. In 1965, there were nearly a million and a half commercial farms with annual sales of less than $10,000; incomes from these farms were half of gross, or less—not much above the poverty line at best, and far below it in many cases. To these very small commercial farms must be added a million noncommercial farms; a few of these were part-time farms, whose operators had good personal incomes, but most were either small part-time farms whose operators earned comparatively little from off-farm work or "retirement" farms, meaning simply that the operator was 65 years old or older and that gross farm output was small (figure 16). These small commercial and noncommercial farms make only a small contribution to agricultural output and provide a poor living for their operators, most of whom are unable to shift to other employments. A disproportionately large number

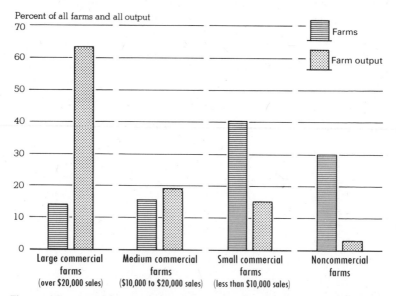

Figure 16. In 1965, total farm output was divided unevenly among the various categories of farms. About one-seventh of the largest farms produced well over half the total output. Nearly a million and a half small commercial farms had gross sales of less than $10,000; as net incomes were only about one-half that figure, many operators were at about the poverty line.

of such farmers are found in Appalachia and in the Ozarks, and throughout the South generally; but some are found in every agricultural county. Poverty is twice as common in rural as in urban areas, and farms contribute their full share to it.

Another by-product of the agricultural revolution has been the social and economic decline of rural communities and small towns dependent upon agriculture. In the day of horse-drawn vehicles, the farmer bought his farm supplies, his groceries, his clothing, and other consumption goods in nearby towns; he often went to a rural church, and his children walked to the little red schoolhouse at the crossroads. Today, in the time his city brother normally spends in daily commuting, he can drive his auto over paved roads many miles to a larger town or city. Rural churches have nearly disappeared; one-room schools have nearly disappeared and children are bussed to consolidated schools; and shopping is at the supermarket, not at the small general store. This has all been part of the revolution in way of life and part of the increasing affluence of the American people—inevitable, perhaps, and mostly good in my scale of values. These changes have left a great many rural communities and small farming towns without any real economic or social role. Many have suffered declines in population, most have lost many of their young people to the larger cities, and many of those that still appear vital are in effect old folks homes for retired and aged farmers.

No one familiar with agriculture thinks that the technological revolution for American agriculture has run its course. Further major changes seem certain, but the long-run future of agricultural production methodology and of rural life is unclear.

## PUBLIC PROGRAMS FOR AGRICULTURE

Agriculture has had a wider variety of federal programs than almost any other sector of the American economy and society. For nearly 100 years there have been educational and research programs at the land-grant colleges and the U.S. Department of Agriculture; for more than 50 years there have been special vocational training programs in high schools and special adult education programs (Agricultural Extension); there have been laws regulating trade in agricultural commodities or establishing grading systems for them, and laws giving agricultural cooperative marketing associations special tax treatment and special immunity from antitrust laws; and there have been large investments made in rural roads, rural electric power lines, and other rural services. Many of these programs have benefited consumers as much as farmers. All of them have affected agricultural land use—sometimes directly but more often indirectly. The agricultural research programs, for example, prepared the way for the agricultural revolution.

Since the 1930s, however, the dominant federal programs have been ones directly affecting cropland use, prices of agricultural commodities, and farm incomes. The post-World War I economic depression was unusually swift and severe, and fell with particular hardship on farmers, especially since transportation and marketing costs remained largely fixed. A cry for "farm relief" went up; and Congress began to consider various programs for controlling surpluses and stabilizing prices of farm commodities. After several years of debate, Congress passed the McNary-Haugen Farm Relief Bill, which was vetoed by President Coolidge in 1927 and again in 1928 on grounds that it contained a price-fixing principle and benefited special groups. In 1929, the Agricultural Marketing Act was passed and the Federal Farm Board was set up. Its approach was "orderly marketing," which was never defined but presumably meant holding back supplies when prices were low. Its prime mechanism was agricultural cooperatives, to which the Farm Board loaned relatively large sums to support the prices of farm commodities. The program began at a particularly inauspicious time; the depression of the 1930s arrived almost simultaneously, and prices of farm commodities plunged downward to levels previously believed impossible. What had seemed like conservative loans quickly became larger than the market value of the commodities. The Farm Board exhausted its funds, the cooperatives were hopelessly in its debt, and in 1933 the Board went out of existence.

The coming of the New Deal in early 1933 marked the beginning of a sharply different approach, which has continued with only modest modifications until the present. Direct efforts at production control were begun; farmers were paid to reduce their crop acreages; prices of farm commodities were supported by loans, and surpluses put into storage. A trinity of production control, price support, and surplus storage became enthroned. At various times, quantities in storage became burdensomely expensive. It not only costs money to store wheat, corn, cotton, butter, and other commodities; there is likely to be some loss in storage, and the stored commodities are always a black cloud hanging over the market. The surpluses that accumulated in the late 1930s and again by 1950 were worked off by the wartime demands of World War II and the Korean War. By the late 1950s surpluses were again at very expensive levels, and in the early 1960s greater financial inducements were held out to farmers to reduce their crop acreages. Crop acreage declined by 50 million acres, and the surpluses were once again reduced to tolerable levels. There has been some shift from price-support to income-support programs under which the farmer gets a direct income payment and prices of commodities are allowed to fall to—or nearer—a competitive market level.

The agricultural programs of the past three decades sought to adjust agricultural output to effective demand at prices higher than the uncontrolled market would have produced. They were concerned solely with area of land used for crops. Other inputs into the productive process were left uncontrolled; fertilizer use increased, crops were shifted to the better lands, larger machinery was used, other new techniques were adopted, and total farm output continued to mount. Moreover, the federal government was not consistent, even in the use of land. Various "conservation" payments were made to help farmers use limestone, or to drain their land or otherwise to increase the productive capacity of their land; other programs brought irrigation water to previously uncropped land, at high subsidy, or provided a degree of flood protection (also at high subsidy) that enabled more intensive cropping of land previously subject to floods. The federal government was like an automobile driver with one foot on the gas and the other on the brake; even the Secretary of Agriculture was in the same position.

These agricultural programs have been expensive. Total appropriations for the U.S. Department of Agriculture have run in the range of $6 billion to $7 billion in recent years; some of this, of course, would continue if all efforts at income support were abandoned. The appropriations to the United States Department of Agriculture are in the general magnitude of $2,000 per farm; only part of this is in the form of direct payments to farmers, part is in storage and other costs of excess supplies, and part is administrative costs. It is also noteworthy that average net income from farming for all farms (part-time, part-retirement, small commercial, large commercial, all averaged together) has been in the range of $4,000 to $5,000 annually in recent years. It is no wonder that some critics are saying, half seriously, that the U.S. Department of Agriculture should be abolished and its appropriations split equally among all farmers.

The programs covering production control, price (or income) support, and surplus storage were designed to help the commercial farmers, especially the larger ones. The direct payments to farmers have shown a few very large payments and many small ones. Any approach to the farm problem that tried to work through market prices of farm commodities or through income support geared to volume of farm output would have shown a similar distribution of benefits. Only the larger farmers have a large enough volume of output to obtain much benefit from higher prices of farm commodities; for many small farmers, no reasonable increase in the prices of commodities they sell would increase their income to a satisfactory level. The programs that were designed to help small farmers have been weak, poorly funded, subject to program revision at frequent intervals, and generally ineffective.

The income support to agriculture has had the further effect of stimulating increases in farm land prices (figure 17). Prices of land in farms, in growing suburban areas, and in recreation use have all moved up rapidly in the past 20 years. Rising prices of farmland are traditionally supposed to make it more difficult for young farmers to get started and to benefit established farmers, who can then retire in their old age out of the increased value of their farms. But in recent years even this supposed advantage to older farmers has been lacking. The average farmer has doubled

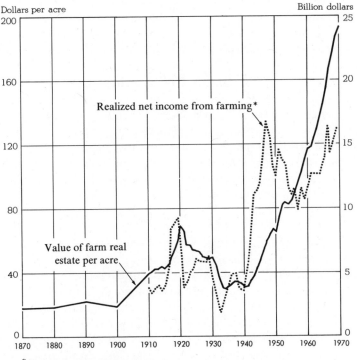

Dollars per acre

Billion dollars

Realized net income from farming*

Value of farm real
estate per acre

* *Including government payments*

Figure 17. Farmers prospered during World War II and the Korean War years, but since the mid-1950s farm incomes have risen less than farm real estate prices.

his land area in the past 20 to 30 years, but what he gained in increased market value of the land he owned, he lost in the price he had to pay for the land he bought. With a total farm real estate value of over $200 billion in the United States today, a reasonable interest return (no more than 6 percent—surely low for 1970 money conditions) eats up nearly all the $13 billion– $16 billion realized net income from farming, leaving very little for labor earnings. Many farmers today have a competitive return for their labor only if they are willing to forgo a competitive return for their capital, and vice versa. Farming has become a high-investment and low-wage industry.

For many years, federal appropriations for agriculture exceeded those for health or education or for urban housing or urban welfare programs, in spite of the fact that the total number of people in agriculture—not just those within agriculture who benefited by the agricultural programs—was much smaller than the number that might have benefited from comparable expenditures in cities. The agricultural programs have become increasingly indefensible, and increasingly under attack. While the programs are strongly entrenched and congressmen from rural districts hold powerful positions in Congress, due in considerable part to the seniority rules, the time may well be coming when major changes in the federal agricultural programs will be forced by urban congressmen.

### Agriculture for the Next Generation

American agriculture is now overmanned with about 3 million farmers, when 1 million or fewer could produce all the commodities we need. It has developed an unbalanced age structure, as young men have sought other employment and left farming increasingly to older men; it has an artificial capital structure, with real estate values that cannot be supported out of current income; it is heavily dependent upon federal government programs to support the prices of its output and the incomes of its farmers; and it is surrounded by rural communities in serious social and economic decline. Agriculture has undergone major technologic, economic, and social changes during the past generation; all signs point to even more drastic changes in the next generation.

What can and should be the form of agriculture and of rural life a generation from now? Shall we let "natural" forces determine its trends and its structure in the future, or should an attempt be made to define an economic and social structure more acceptable to our standards? In other words, shall we be "trend-acceptors" or "trend-benders"? If we should decide that the trends now apparent will lead to an agriculture and a rural life less than ideal, how do we go about effectively changing these trends? Is this any real concern to the urban man of the future? Or will he wash his hands of agriculture's problems?

# CHAPTER SIX

# Grazing Land

One of the largest uses of land in the United States is the grazing of domestic livestock on natural forages (or closely related permanently seeded areas, in a few cases). This is the chief use of 640 million acres of land (see figure 1 and table 7). In addition, 224 million acres that are classified as chiefly forested provide some grazing. About three-fourths of the land in each category is privately owned, and about a fourth is publicly owned (mostly by the federal government). The total is an immense territory, almost 40 percent of the whole area of the United States. About 85 percent of this large area lies in the Great Plains and the West; in these regions, grazing is by far the largest user of land.

Grazing and rangeland, both privately and publicly owned, is used by livestock owned by private individuals. Some of these will be called farmers, if they primarily grow crops and only incidentally run livestock on the ranges; others will be called ranchers, if their chief agricultural activity is livestock raising by grazing rather than by feeding of harvested crops. There is no sharp or clear line between farms and ranches; it is a matter of degree of dependence not only upon livestock but also upon grazing of native plants.

TABLE 7. LAND USED PRIMARILY OR PARTLY FOR PASTURE
AND RANGE, BY OWNERSHIP CATEGORY, 1964

*(million acres)*

| Land use | Privately owned | Publicly owned | Total |
|----------|---------|---------|-------|
| Land used primarily for pasture and range | 482 | 159 | 641 |
| Forested land also used for pasture and range | 161 | 63 | 224 |
| Total | 643 | 222 | 865 |

Grazing is the use of this land largely by default. Most of the land used for grazing is too dry, too steep, or too rocky or has too shallow soils to grow crops; and the land that is used primarily as range will support few, if any, trees. Various kinds of native grasses, shrubs, and annual forbs or weeds grow naturally. In some favored spots, public agencies or ranchers have seeded permanent grasses, either native or introduced species such as wheat grasses. Livestock grazing has sometimes altered the plant composition by greater removal of some species than others; and white men control fires on range areas, whereas Indians often used fire to affect growth of grass and hence distribution of game animals; as a result today the plant cover may be substantially different than it was when domestic livestock first began grazing on the area. Ranchers and public agencies have constructed water improvements in many areas, enabling the domestic animals to make a more intensive utilization of the native forage than the game animals ever could. Moreover, by growing cultivated crops for livestock feed during winter or other seasons of scarce natural feed, ranchers have enabled their livestock to survive and hence to make a heavier utilization of the range than the wild animals could; numbers of the latter were often kept in check by severe winters, droughts, and other natural phenomena from which Man has largely sheltered his domestic animals. Many grazing lands are only seasonally useful; high mountain areas, for instance, may provide good summer grazing but will be covered by deep snow in winter.

These natural ranges produce relatively little usable forage per acre. Only the best ranges produce as much as 1,000 pounds of natural forage annually; the average is far lower than this, and many of the poorer ranges produce less than a tenth as much. Wild or natural hay, when harvested, usually yields about a ton per acre, worth in recent years about $15 to $20 per ton. Thus, range is materially less productive than the least-productive harvested cropland that it most closely resembles. At such a low output per acre, it would not pay Man to harvest the forage himself; however, the grazing animals can do this naturally and efficiently. Moreover, by keeping considerable numbers of livestock and grazing them over large acreages of land, a rancher can produce as much economic output *per man* as a good farmer can on some of the better cropland. A good-sized, one-man cattle ranch may well have 400 head of cattle, and may use 15,000 to 20,000 acres or more of private and public land for grazing and feed producing.

A really skillful rancher is a practicing ecologist. He cannot afford to spend much in improving range lands, even the better ones; he must learn to manage in such a way that the livestock can harvest as much of the forage growth as possible without destroying the ability of the forage plants not only to survive but to reproduce and flourish. This requires that he graze the ranges at the proper season, with not excessive numbers of livestock, without excessive concentrations of stock in favored spots, with rest for the range seasonally or in some years, and with other good management measures. Needless to say, not all ranchers are this skillful. In an earlier day, many seriously overused their ranges, or used them at wrong seasons, or made no provision for letting some areas grow to the point where the plants produced seed, or otherwise misused their land. On private ranges, this was often due to lack of information about good range management; on some public land it was for many years due to a lack of control over grazing use—if one man did not graze his livestock until all the forage was consumed, another would.

## How Grazing Land Developed in American History

One cannot understand present use of grazing land without some history of its development. There was always some grazing of livestock on the frontier, from the earliest colonial times. Oaks and other trees provided rich food, as did grasses and various herbaceous plants. These could be harvested economically only by the livestock themselves; and the livestock could furnish their own motive power to get to market. Indians were a constant hazard until the end of the nineteenth century. At times of Indian trouble, the cattle herders would withdraw to the settlements, either taking their livestock with them, or hoping the animals would escape. When conditions quieted down, the frontier cattlemen would move farther out. Until after the Civil War, this type of livestock production took place on a thin band of land, usually not more than 20 miles wide, along the settled frontier. But after the Civil War, venturesome cattlemen moved out onto the Great Plains and into the Rocky Mountains. Surplus cattle were driven north from Texas, grazed upon the plains, and shipped to eastern markets over the new railroads. Breeding herds were established in the new regions. In less than 15 years after the war ended, virtually all the western half of the nation had herds of cattle or flocks of sheep grazing at some season.

At first, this ranching industry was almost wholly on public land. No man owned it, every man had an equal legal right to graze upon it. These were the circumstances out of which the range wars arose. The strongest claimant, in an era when law and order were often lacking, was able to appropriate the range to his temporary use. But gradually the homesteaders came—some genuinely seeking land for farming, and some only seeking to obtain title to land so that they could sell it—and the ranchers were forced to obtain title to substantial areas of land. Almost all the grazing land in the plains, and irrigated meadows, waterholes, and key ranges in the mountain regions moved into private ownership. This left the mountain regions with extensive areas of federal land most of which is in national forests and grazing districts today.

Once the rancher owned the land his animals grazed upon, he found it necessary to modify his methods of livestock production. The early ranching industry was based wholly upon grazing; no hay, grain, or other feeds were harvested for winter feeding. During mild winters, this was satisfactory. But when a severe winter came, as it inevitably did, the outcome was a tragic loss of livestock and financial failure for many operators. The legend of the "hard winter" is part of the culture of every ranching area. Ranchers were forced to cut wild hay for winter feeding, or to cultivate land for other feed crops. The type of livestock produced also underwent major change. The early Texas Longhorn was a gaunt, ungainly creature, with wide, sweeping horns, able

to travel far and long for water or grass, but it was neither efficient as a gainer nor delectable as beef. Improved strains of
various breeds transformed the kind of livestock raised in the
latter years of the nineteenth century and the early years of the
twentieth. Improvement is still going on.

The early grazing industry was, almost without exception,
highly exploitive in nature. For the most part, ranchers moved
from areas of moderate rainfall into drier areas. They knew little
about the climate and ecology of the regions into which they
moved, and they seriously overestimated the capacity of the new
ranching lands to produce forage and to regenerate under severe
grazing pressure. The fact that the lands were not their own
made planning for the future impossible; they used the grass and
moved on. Since the early grazing lands were typically plowed
for crop farming within a few years, it did not matter if the
grazing capacity of the ranges was seriously depleted. These early
experiences led to some damage to the range areas; they also
built up attitudes in the minds of ranchers that made conservation and sustained use more difficult to achieve.

Ranchers have been widely criticized by conservationists for
their exploitive use of range lands. It is true that use was commonly excessive, especially in the early decades. But exploitation
of natural resources—either with little concern for the future or
with little knowledge of the consequences of actions taken—was
by no means confined to ranchers. It was common among farmers
and among forest industries as well. A lack of knowledge of the
new environment and a persistent tendency to overestimate its
capabilities has characterized the settlement and development of
the North American continent. Someone has said that a pioneer
was an optimist, or he was not a pioneer.

In the last generation, ranchers, like farmers and forest users,
have learned vastly more about the conservation and sustained
use of their resources. Economic conditions and public programs
alike have provided major incentives to use rangeland at an
intensity that can be maintained. Much rangeland is still being
improperly grazed, but notable progress has been made in in-
stituting grazing practices that do not destroy the productivity of
the land, and further progress seems clearly probable.

NATURAL CONDITIONS OF THE RANGE REGION

Although the grazing areas are alike in not being suited for cultivated crops, they differ greatly in their natural vegetation and in their response to grazing of domestic animals. There are a wide variety of natural grasses, with different requirements of temperature, moisture, and soil conditions. Some grasses grow best during relatively cool seasons, while others thrive on warm seasons; some grow relatively tall, often in clumps or bunches (some are known as bunch grasses), while others are low or close-growing; some are annuals, others are perennials. Some of the perennial grasses have long roots that enable them to draw moisture from deep in the soil and they can withstand rather severe droughts. Some of the annuals are very prolific seed producers; the seeds sprout and grow when moisture conditions are favorable, but lie dormant for long periods when moisture is unavailable. Then there is a wide variety of shrubs: great sagebrush and other shrubs, classed as northern desert shrubs by the range managers; and saltbush and other shrubs classed as southern desert shrubs. And in the pinion-juniper areas, which are characterized by rather sparse stands of these two low-growing trees, there are understories of sagebrush, some lower shrubs, and grasses.

Other special forage types are found in the higher mountains. There are grassy mountain meadows, often highly productive but vulnerable to overuse; aspen and associated tree types, with varying amounts and kinds of low-growing forage plants; and open ponderosa pine stands, often very beautiful, with modest growths of shrubs and grasses. There are some dense forests, but these are usually not good grazing areas for either livestock or game animals because the trees shade out the growth of forage plants. There are also desert areas with a sparse growth of low shrubs, where sheep graze during the winter when the scant snow cover provides some water.

The range areas, reaching from the Mexican to the Canadian border and varying greatly in elevation and in climate, naturally produced a great variety of plant associations. Grazing itself has modified the original plant cover. In a sagebrush-grass range, for instance, the livestock consume the grass readily and the sagebrush sparingly; if grazing is too intensive, the grass is weakened, the sagebrush responds to the reduced competition for the limited moisture supply, and the range becomes more heavily sagebrush. In many areas, junipers, which were always part of the natural scene, have been increasing in recent decades, partly as a result of reduced competition from the grasses for moisture and partly as a result of fire protection (the trees were more vulnerable to fires than the grasses). In still other areas, mesquite (a very hardy but unpalatable shrub) has formed dense thickets, as grass has been reduced in vigor or eliminated. Some of these trends have been reversed in recent years as ranchers or public agencies have used fire or bulldozers to eliminate all or most of the shrubs, and have planted grass—either an introduced species, such as crested wheatgrass, or native grasses.

Because much of the range is only seasonally usable, an intricate pattern of seasonal use has emerged. This is illustrated in figure 18, although the situation is more complicated than can be shown on a map of this scale. The Great Plains is shown as yearlong range, for instance, and cattle are indeed grazed throughout the year; but many ranchers save some pastures for spring grazing, some for summer grazing, and still others for winter; or they may produce some harvested crops for winter feeding (even when forage has been saved for this season) , so that they will have feed if the weather is too cold for grazing. In the mostly winter range areas, which are used primarily by sheep in winter, there may be a few cattle ranchers who graze their livestock more or less all year. Much of the summer range is sharply limited to summer use, because of winter snows, but there are variations even here.

The domestic livestock must have feed every day in the year; the rancher's job is to provide that feed, either as grazing or in the form of harvested crops, as economically as he can, and in such a way that the productivity of the range is preserved over a period of years. Some land best suited for spring and fall grazing may have to be used as summer range, because the latter is in scarce supply within reasonable distance of his ranch headquarters; or some land not well-suited for spring and fall grazing

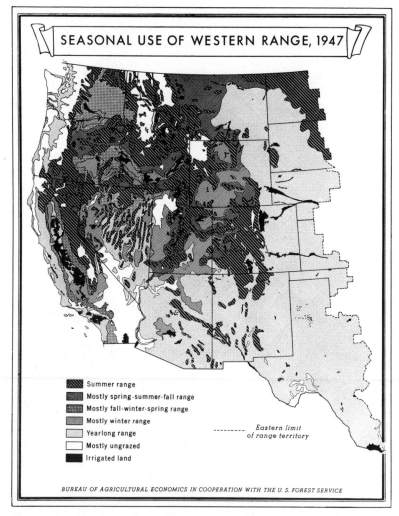

Figure 18.   Because much rangeland is only usable at certain times of the year, the pattern of seasonal use is an intricate one.

may nevertheless have to be used in these seasons because of a general shortage of spring and fall range in that locality. What the rancher can afford to pay for grazing privileges, or what he can afford to invest in developing otherwise unproductive or unusable range, or what he can afford to spend to produce harvested forage crops, thus depends in part upon the abundance or scarcity of range forage at various seasons.

The amount of forage produced by grazing regions varies considerably from year to year, and from season to season. In large part, this is due to variations in precipitation, since most of the grazing country is short of moisture. Feed production may vary from half or less of average to twice or more—not enough some seasons, more than the livestock can eat at others. Moreover, these variations may continue for several seasons; periods as long as 10 years may average 25 percent or more above or below a truly long-term average. The most extreme weather events are drought and severe winters. In drought, there simply is not enough moisture for much plant growth; unless domestic animals are moved elsewhere quickly, or are provided supplementary feed, they will die, as they did in the very severe droughts of 1934 and 1936. In an extreme winter when snow covers such forage as exists, many animals will perish unless they are provided with harvested feed. These natural weather variations helped to keep game animals in check and prevent their overgrazing of the ranges; Man has softened the shock of adverse weather situations on his domestic animals, and thus weakened the natural checks upon overgrazing.

THE HEALTH OF THE RANGE

Grazing areas have had a somewhat similar history to that of cropland areas, as far as erosion and depletion are concerned. The progression of settlement from humid to dry areas tended to mislead ranchers about the capacity of the rangeland to bear up under heavy use. Their lack of knowledge about the effects of grazing upon the vegetation was one of the major factors in the overuse and misuse of the land; lack of control during the public land period was another.

Although a Forest Service report on range conditions in 1936 indicated that there was still a downward trend, the low point in range condition was probably reached about the same time as that for cropland—roughly, during the 1920s. In retrospect, it seems clear that the authors of the Forest Service report were unduly influenced by the severe drought conditions of the time, even though an effort had been made to make allowance for abnormal weather conditions. The report aroused a lot of interest among conservationists, while ranchers took exception to the tone as well as the facts.

The national forests were brought under grazing management before World War I, but major adjustments in livestock numbers continued almost steadily until 1950 and smaller ones until the present. In 1934, the Taylor Grazing Act provided a means for administering grazing on the remaining public land. The initiation of soil conservation programs about the same date provided technical assistance in erosion control and in management.

A new era in grazing land use began in the mid-1930s. Since then, there has been substantial improvement in the management of both publicly and privately owned grazing land and hence in the health of grazing land. Much rangeland today is in about as good shape as it can be, given the natural conditions, and much is managed well and productively. At the same time, a great deal of range is in poor condition, some is still deteriorating, and much is less productive than it might be. As with cropland, one cannot fairly overlook either the progress that has been made or the improvements yet needed. Sometimes, range restoration proceeds slowly, even under the best of conditions, primarily because of climatic situations. Many ranges were ecologically brittle, and past changes cannot be reversed easily or quickly—or, in some cases, perhaps ever. One of the heartening aspects is the greatly increased awareness and knowledge of ranchers; some younger ones, college-trained, are as capable range managers as the public agency personnel.

## THE FUTURE OF GRAZING AREAS

Beef is the major output of grazing areas; lamb and wool are of less, though still considerable, importance. Beef is much in demand in the United States, and, as incomes rise, people tend to consume more beef or are willing to pay higher prices for it, or both. As total population in the United States increases over the next decades, total beef consumption will surely rise considerably. Only some of the increase will be met by ranches. Beef can also be produced on farms—in fact, far more is produced there than from grazing lands. It may be that beef can be produced more cheaply on farms with cultivated crops and improved pastures. However, many possibilities still remain for increased forage production from grazing areas by improvements such as reseeding or brush clearing and by better range management. Ranchers, like farmers, are under some economic pressure to adopt new production practices.

The grazing of domestic animals on range or grazing areas is thus likely to continue, more or less as it has in the past, with some improvements and some increased output per unit of land. When rangeland is in demand for other uses, and suitable for them, it will almost surely be taken for such uses. But the extent of such adjustments will probably be small compared with the really vast area of grazing land.

One likely change is that more and more ranches will be operated as a sideline instead of as a prime source of living. The public sees ranching as agriculture's glamour industry; one need only observe how many television programs are based upon the myths of the cowboy, the range war, and the gun battle to see how true this is. Many men of wealth, or near wealth, seem to hanker to own a ranch; and in buying ranches they have generally bid up the prices of ranch and range property to levels where the turnoff of beef or other products from the ranch cannot hope to pay wages and earn interest on the investment.

As one contemplates the future, the possibilities of using both public and private grazing land for purposes other than grazing must be considered. One likely use is for recreation, an activity that is already spreading onto desert and other areas where once it would have seemed a strange or inappropriate use. Grazing lands now provide an opportunity for hunting, but this is basically a nonexclusive use (although careless hunters sometimes make the range dangerous for man and beast). Hunting will almost surely continue and may grow in importance; but, by and large, the grazing areas are not attractive outdoor recreation areas. This is especially true for the plains and the desert valleys and foothills. The high mountains are another story, and many mountain meadows are likely to be converted from grazing to recreation areas. Outdoor recreation is thus likely to have some, though limited, impact on grazing land use.

The importance of many grazing areas as watersheds may well increase in the future, especially as population rises in the more arid western regions and the competition for water increases. Many grazing areas yield relatively small amounts of water, but contribute disproportionately to the volume of sediments in the water. In some of the dry ranges, from which a good deal of sediment now originates, reduction in grazing may be a necessary means of erosion control. In some of the higher mountain areas now used for grazing, there are possibilities for modifying or increasing the water yield through vegetative manipulation; however, this method is as likely to increase as decrease the forage available to domestic livestock, because vegetative manipulation often means the replacement of trees by shrubs and grasses. While watershed considerations are likely to override grazing considerations, it would appear that the impact upon total usable forage production will not be great.

If one takes a longer look ahead, two unusual uses might arise on present grazing lands, neither of which would take large areas. First of all, there might be an attempt to build one or more new towns in present grazing areas; the openness of the landscape and the lack of many competing land uses would be an attraction, but it is doubtful that this advantage would offset other problems in such locations—and the problems of new towns are difficult enough at best, as noted in the chapter on urban land. Another new use of present grazing land might be as waste disposal areas for cities—large-scale but distant garbage dumps. This might take the form of landfill for urban solid wastes; a proposal of this kind was advanced in California a few years ago, but it fell through when a cheaper site was found. Industries with a waste disposal problem might be attracted to range areas, especially those in closed basins where there would be no drainage to downstream areas or to the sea. Such uses would indeed be different and they might be highly important to the affected areas, but they would not take any really significant part of the present grazing area.

# CHAPTER SEVEN

# *Forests*

Nearly all of the United States east of the Mississippi River and extensive areas west of it were naturally forested when the European colonists first began settlements here. These forests were rather complex ecosystems, usually with two or more major tree species, often with several lesser trees, shrubs, and other plants, and a complex of animal and bird life. By and large, these forests contained as much wood as the soil and climate would support; they were "mature," or "virgin," or "storage," depending upon the term one prefers. As old or damaged trees died, fell down, and rotted, new ones took their place; on the whole, there was no net growth.

The early colonists were amazed at the variety of trees and at the size of individual trees, also at the wonderful clear lumber they made. The volume of wood per acre was far beyond anything they had known, or imagined, before they came. The pines of New England made such superb masts for the sailing vessels of the day that Britain was anxious to have such masts for its own ships and to keep other nations from getting them. Colonists were forbidden to cut pines on which the King's Arrow had been carved by British government men; such trees were reserved for sale only to the British navy. The colonists then, like settlers on the frontier for two centuries or more later, ignored government restrictions when they could and wished to do so.

The forests provided building material and fuel for the colonists. They were therefore a great asset, but they also presented a major problem. If crops were to be grown, the forest had to be cleared and, even when the tools were available, the colonists found this a slow and difficult task. Moreover, the forests hid the Indians who at times swooped down upon the settlements. The colonists' view of the forests was thus ambivalent.

These early forests were penetrable only on foot or on horseback, and then only by following trails that Indians had long used. Since a man could travel through densely treed areas for days on end, one can understand how the terms "endless" and "inexhaustible" came to be applied to these forests. Colonists could hardly visualize a time when forests might become scarce and valuable, although sources of fuel and building materials closely accessible to the towns did in fact become scarce by the time of the Revolution. But the term and the idea of inexhaustibility continued to be widely accepted until at least the end of the nineteenth century. If the natural forests were truly inexhaustible, why should one seek to grow trees for future lumber supplies, or even care much whether the natural forests replenished themselves? This attitude was a bar to better management of forested lands for a very long time.

A BRIEF FOREST HISTORY

The original forests were cut about as rapidly as the settlers could do so. In a great many areas, of which Ohio is a good example, the forests were cut and the trees burned in place to clear the land for farming; such trees as were needed by the settler were naturally used by him, but his needs were small and he had no way of marketing what he did not use himself. Other forests were cut and the logs converted into lumber; the great centers of logging moved from Maine into the northern Lake States, then into the South, and finally to the Pacific Northwest. Harvesting methods were designed to get out the usable logs, without concern about what was left. Little or no attempt was made to control fires, and no steps were taken to encourage new growth, partly because there was a general belief that the land would be converted into farms. Unfortunately, it was soon demonstrated that much of the land was unsuitable for farming.

In the early days, logs were "driven" down the streams during the spring floods and then converted into lumber. Other means of transportation were lacking, and other uses of logs unknown. Much later, the logging railroad opened up many areas that could not readily be harvested by floating out the logs because the streams were too small or too remote; and still later, well after World War I, the tractor and the truck opened up still other areas and provided more economical ways of getting logs out. In this later period, wood fiber came increasingly to be used to make paper and for plywood. Lumber production hit a peak before World War I, which it has never exceeded since; but plywood and paper production are still rising steeply, and are likely to continue to do so.

The cutting of a virgin forest was a shock to its ecosystem; burning was a further severe shock. Some forests were able to restock themselves; but more often, other kinds of trees grew back at first. In the course of time, the original species composition and kind of stand might be reestablished; but this might take hundreds of years. The same natural conditions that produced the original forests will nearly always restore some kind of a forest cover; in nearly all the originally forested area, abandoned farmland naturally grows up to forest. The first growth may be primarily shrubs; these are followed by various tree species that shade and crowd out the shrubs; and these trees in turn are superseded by still other tree species. The resulting forest may not be economically productive for a long time, but it, too, is a complex ecosystem. Forests from which all economically usable trees have been harvested are often called "degraded" by foresters, but they are often open in character, which may actually make them more attractive for outdoor recreation than the dense original forest, and they may provide more feed for a wider variety of game animals.

By the middle of the nineteenth century, some thoughtful people were alarmed at the forest destruction and the lack of productive regrowth. For many years, increasing concern was expressed, and in 1891, the first "forest reserves" (now the national forests) were established. The program of permanent retention of forest lands in federal ownership, initiated at this time, was largely completed before World War I. At first, the management of these lands was custodial; fires were kept out or put out, instead of being allowed to burn themselves out, and trespass timber cutting was reduced greatly. Standing timber was available for sale to interested private buyers, but total sales were low until World War II. There was simply too much privately owned timber, often more accessible, which the owners were anxious to convert into salable products, for there to be much sale of public timber. The importance of the federal timber has changed enormously in recent years.

During much of the early period, the timber industry removed as much timber as it could from public lands, taking it without authority and in trespass. When necessary, lumbermen bought public domain lands—either directly from the government or from individuals who had acquired them—harvested the timber quickly, and abandoned the lands. As prices for lumber and other forest products were low, there was no financial incentive to grow trees or to own forests for their long-term productive capacity. Up until the end of World War II, a great many lumber producers owned little or no timberland of their own; they depended on buying logs from government agencies or from private individuals. But some companies acquired some of the most productive forest lands while they were still available, and the beginnings of some of the present large forest holdings trace back to 1900 or earlier. As the processing of wood became more complex and was carried further in terms of final product, the large processors wanted to own at least part of their timber supply as a protection for their processing investment.

Another major feature of forest history was the rise of forestry as a profession: there were few trained foresters in 1900; today there are many. Forestry, like agriculture, is no longer a place for the untrained manager.

## Forest Landownership and Management Today

Excluding productive forests reserved for various purposes, such as parks, the Forest Service found 743 million acres of forest land in 1963 (the latest year for which complete data have been published); 508 million acres of this land were commercial forest land, and the rest was noncommercial (the dividing line between commercial and noncommercial being determined by economic as well as physical conditions). Nearly three-fourths of the total forest land was in the East and only a fourth in the

West. Only about 41 percent of the commercial forest land supported stands of sawtimber size; the remaining area had smaller
trees or was nonstocked. The total forest lands supported about
700 billion cubic feet of timber, or roughly 1,000 feet per acre;
considerably more than half of this total volume was in the sawlog portions of the trees in sawtimber stands. Slightly more than
half of the total timber volume was in the West, where some old
growth forests have not yet been cut, and where there are many
types of forests that tend to support higher volumes than the
typical forests of the East.

For all forests in the United States, annual growth in 1962 was
1.6 times annual cut. This is a great reversal from the situation
a few decades ago. During the long period of harvesting mature
or virgin stands, annual cut far exceeded annual growth, and
timber inventory steadily declined. Some of the actual decline
was obscured because successive inventories of "commercial"
timber included trees that would not have been so classified
earlier. The low point in timber inventory may have been
reached in the late 1930s or the 1940s—the same general period,
it will be recalled, when cropland erosion was at its worst and
when range condition was at its lowest. By 1952, total growth
was 1.3 times total cut. The fact that growth has exceeded cut
for the past two decades or longer is heartening, but its sig-
nificance should not be exaggerated. Much of the growth is in
small-size trees, not always of the best quality or the most
desired species, while the cut is overwhelmingly in mature trees,
the best yet available. Moreover, there is a regional disparity;
growth far exceeds cut in the East, while cut still exceeds growth
in the West. Nevertheless, if the favorable relationship between
growth and cut continues to improve, as is altogether possible,
the outlook for a continued supply of timber would also
improve.

Data on acreage, sawtimber volume, number of ownerships,
and productivity are shown in figure 19 for public, forest industry, farm, and "other" commercial forests. In 1963, the latest
date for which information is available, the acreage was distributed as follows: (1) public, 142 million acres, of which
federal land is about 80 percent; (2) forest industry (both pulp

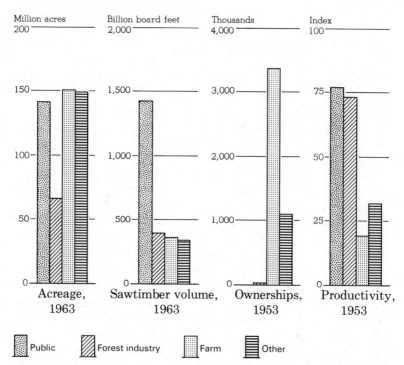

| Million acres | Billion board feet | Thousands | Index |
| 200 | 2,000 | 4,000 | 100 |

Acreage, 1963 · Sawtimber volume, 1963 · Ownerships, 1953 · Productivity, 1953

Public · Forest industry · Farm · Other

Figure 19. Well over half the sawtimber volume in 1963 was found on public forests, much of it on the national forests, and the proportion is at least as high today. Public and forest-industry forests are about on a par in terms of productivity. Farm and other forests are extensive in area, low in timber volume, and tend to be relatively unproductive.

and paper and lumber), 67 million acres; (3) farm, 151 million acres; and (4) miscellaneous private, 149 million acres. The 1963 survey did not include information on numbers of forest ownerships in each category, hence no data on average size of ownership, but the 1953 survey did include such information. In 1953 there were less than 24,000 forest industry ownerships, averaging about 2,700 acres each; there were nearly 3½ million farm ownerships, averaging less than 50 acres each; and 1.1 million miscellaneous private ownerships, averaging about 120 acres each. (It is not meaningful to show *number* of public ownerships. As noted above, 80 percent of the public land is owned by the federal government; the rest is owned by states.) The situation has probably changed somewhat since 1953 for farm forests; since there are far fewer farms today, because farms have been consolidated into fewer but larger units, there are also fewer farm forests of somewhat larger average size. Farm forests are still small; most are simply woodlots on land not suitable for farming or not worth clearing, and the farmer neglects them most of the time.

The great importance of publicly owned forest lands is apparent from their stocking with sawlog timber. Well over half of all sawtimber in 1963 was found on public forests, much of it on the national forests; the proportion is at least as high today. Even this comparison understates the importance of the public forests, for their sawtimber is larger and of higher quality than much of that on other lands. From data assembled by the Forest Service in 1953, I have constructed an index of forest productivity. On this basis, the public and forest industry forests were on a par; far behind them were the "other" forests, and bringing up the rear were the farm forests (see figure 19). Similar information is not available in the 1963 forest survey; however, the same general situation still exists. The public forests are as a whole large in area, high in volume of good grade trees, and high in productivity; the forest industry forests are less than half as extensive, have lower volumes of timber because they were more heavily cut in the past, but are in good productive condition in general; the farm and other forests are extensive in area, low in timber volume, and generally relatively unproductive. Many forest industry forests have gone through one or more cuts, and now have second-growth stands; much public forest has never been cut.

The extent of timber stocking is correlated with size of forest holding; the large units are usually well-stocked, while the small units are poorly stocked. This is true within each ownership class, but, since farm and "other" forests average so small, their average condition is also relatively poor. The economic prospects for forests are positively correlated with size of holding (see table 8). On very small holdings it does not pay the operator to spend much time and energy in getting informed about good forestry and land management, nor can such holdings repay much investment in them. The larger forest industry holdings are managed as well as the federal holdings, on the average, and the best ones are managed much better. In this connection, it should be noted that the annual economic output of the average forest acre in the United States is about one-sixth of the comparable output from the average farm acre. Thus, the small farm forests and the miscellaneous private forests are seen to be very small indeed.

Most publicly owned forests are now managed for sustained yield and multiple use. If annual timber harvest for a manage-

TABLE 8. AREA AND ECONOMIC PROSPECTS FOR PRIVATE FORESTS OF DIFFERENT SIZES

| Size of forest tract (acres) | Total acreage in this size class, 1953 (million acres) | Economic prospects for good forestry (based on size alone) |
|---|---|---|
| Over 50,000 | 58 | Good to excellent. |
| 5,000 to 50,000 | 35 | Good. |
| 500 to 5,000 | 46 | Fair to good; most such units are below optimum size to form an economic forest unit by themselves; most require some specialized management in addition to the owner's, but some economic incentives to good forestry do exist on the larger tracts of better site quality. |
| 100 to 500 | 98 | Fair; such forests are usually sidelines to some other economic activity; larger farm forests, if well-stocked, may offer a fair prospect; poorer and smaller farm forests offer very little economic incentive; among "other" forests, the better ones offer some prospects if under some form of group or supervised management. |
| Under 100 | 121 | Poor to nonexistent, except in case of farm forests integrated with agricultural enterprise, or unless combined with other ownerships for management purposes. |

*Source:* Charles H. Stoddard, *The Small Private Forest in the United States* (Washington: Resources for the Future, Inc., 1961), p. 57.

ment area is limited to annual timber growth on that area, then the supply of timber will be continuous and sustained. Under this concept of sustained yield, timber harvest may exceed timber growth on particular tracts in some years as long as the total growth is equal to total harvest. When the forest is used to produce forage for domestic livestock or game animals, or to produce recreation, or is managed for its watershed values as well as for the production of timber products, multiple use management is evident. A particular tract may be used exclusively for one purpose, such as a campground, while the whole forested area is managed for multiple use. Management may be relatively extensive—keeping fires to a minimum, harvesting the growth that grows "naturally," and not much more; or it may be intensive, in varying degrees—planting seeds or seedlings on harvested land that does not quickly and fully reseed naturally, thinning young stands of trees to eliminate weak or slow-growing trees more quickly than natural growth would have shaded them out, even pruning young trees to reduce knots in the mature log at a later date, possibly even fertilizing the forest, controlling insects and tree diseases as far as this is practical, and so on. An additional form of intensive forestry is seeking out markets for the less valuable tree species, sizes, and grades, thus permitting some additional harvest.

Although forestry on public forests is more intensive today than it was a generation ago, there is still room for further improvement. However, there are many obstacles to be overcome. The whole government budget-appropriation-expenditure process is slow and cumbersome; investments are made slowly, the level of expenditure usually lags behind the optimum, and management is not able to take advantage of good opportunities. This is especially serious today, when more than half of all sawtimber is on publicly owned forests (mostly national forests). The volumes of timber on some of these lands are high, compared with the low volumes on much poorly stocked private forests; but growth rates are low, in part because the mature stands are making little or no net growth, but also because cutover areas have not been restocked as rapidly or as completely as they should have been or because growing stands are not managed at their optimum intensity. One of the major problems in forestry for the next decade or two is to find ways to manage the public forests more intensively.

## Some Recent Trends in Forestry

Total consumption of lumber has recently climbed back to about the peak reached before World War I, but population has increased greatly over the years and per capita lumber consumption is much lower than it was at that time. The best outlook is that per capita consumption will continue to decline, but slowly so that total consumption will rise modestly. Lumber is still extremely important in the construction industry. In contrast, both per capita and total consumption of plywood and veneer has risen sharply in the past 30 years or more, and both promise to continue to do so. Likewise, both per capita and total consumption of wood pulp, which is made into paper of various kinds, has risen greatly and promises to continue to rise. The shift has thus been away from the relatively less-processed form of wood fiber (the large, solid sawn pieces) into the more modified sheets and papers. Plywood, for instance, is more flexible than lumber in its proportions and in properties that can be built into it; labor savings in its use may more than offset any greater expenditure in its manufacture. This trend toward more highly processed forms of wood fiber is likely to continue; the next big step would be a major utilization of wood chemicals as building blocks for other products.

One factor underlying these consumption trends has been different trends in product prices. Over a very long time, lumber prices have risen, more or less steadily, in relation to the prices of other commodities. This trend was particularly marked during the 1940s and early 1950s; there followed a period when lumber prices seemed to have more or less stabilized, but in the latter 1960s lumber prices shot up to new levels. In contrast, paper prices have remained reasonably steady, compared with commodities in general, and plywood prices have actually trended downward on the same comparative basis. The increases in lumber prices have been translated back into higher stumpage prices, sometimes more than proportionately, because the costs of harvesting and manufacturing the products have not risen proportionately. Douglas fir stumpage on national forests, for example, sold for about $2.00 per 1,000 board feet prior to World War II but reached $50.02 in 1966—and the latter price was probably for a somewhat lower grade of log in a somewhat more expensive area to harvest. High prices in recent years have led to demands from timber processors that export of logs and/or lumber to other countries, notably Japan, be limited or eliminated.

Before World War II, forest processors often found that it was cheaper to buy logs or standing trees than to own timber-producing land. After the war, however, with the end of mature timber clearly in sight, though not imminent for some years, many processors began buying forest land from smaller owners, especially in the Pacific Northwest where the remaining mature stands were heavily concentrated. As the acreage of independently owned land shrank, the race to buy speeded up; today in the Pacific Northwest, it is nearly impossible to buy private timber unless one buys out the whole operation, including the processing plant, of some other forest industry firm. There has been a notable consolidation or merging of firms, sometimes quite large ones. At the same time, many firms have diversified their operations; by sorting logs according to grade for plywood and lumber, and by using other logs and wastes for pulp production, they can achieve a more efficient utilization of the forest output. All of this is easier for a large firm than for a small firm.

## The Future of Forests

The outlook for the conventional forest products (lumber, plywood, pulp, poles, etc.) can be briefly summarized: (1) total demand for all forest products is projected to be 80 percent higher in 2000 than it was in 1962, when the last thorough Forest Service analysis was made; (2) the supply of such wood products will be adequate until 1980 or 1985, and the situation thereafter will depend in large part upon trends in forest productivity; (3) the average quality of wood products harvested will continue to decline; and (4) the opportunities for more intensive forest management are very great, and such intensive management could greatly increase the forest output and hence affect the supply-demand balance. Since the interval between planting and harvest is so long, even with the more shortened rotations now practiced and probable for the future, a long look ahead is unavoidable for anyone concerned with forestry.

A dominant fact about forests in the United States today is that, as a whole, their productivity is low. In 1962, there was a growth of 16.2 billion cubic feet of wood; the volume of standing growing stock was estimated at 627.9 billion cubic feet; thus, growth in that year was only 2.6 percent of growing stock. To put the same matter differently, the 1962 growth in wood volume was from about 508 million acres, or a growth in volume of only 32 cubic feet per acre. One reason for this low output is the limited natural capacity of the forest lands; it is estimated that about a third have the capacity to produce 85 cubic feet per acre or more annually, but that nearly a fourth have a capacity of less than 50 cubic feet; on this basis, the average productivity is about 75 cubic feet per acre annually, compared with the 32 cubic feet actually produced in 1962. The divergence between actual and potential growth is due primarily to the low stocking on extensive areas and to the general lack of intensive forestry practices. There is little or no net growth on the remaining mature or virgin stands.

In this connection, it must be pointed out that a growing tree is both capital and output. A standing tree represents capital; cutting the tree is a means of translating this semifixed capital into cash. If the tree stands, it adds to its volume annually, the increase in volume in turn becoming more capital. Over the life of a tree, increases in value are proportionate to increases in physical volume; this may not be true during particular parts of the growth cycle—increases in volume have no salable or harvestable value until a tree reaches merchantable size, and at some other stages increases in volume may add more than proportionately to increases in value. With an average annual increase in volume of all standing timber of only 2.6 percent, the increase in value could not have been much greater. If growth could be increased to the estimated capacity of forest land to grow wood, or to about 75 cubic feet annually on the average, the annual growth would increase to 6.1 percent of present volume. To accomplish this would require some reduction in volume of standing timber on the presently mature forest areas and some increase elsewhere, but probably a net decrease in standing volume for all forest land. If so, the annual growth would increase as a percentage of standing volume, to an unknown but probably not major degree. Even if annual growth should reach 8 percent of standing volume, this would not be a high rate of return, considering the risks and the general illiquidity of forest investments.

For a great many forests, a larger economic return may be secured by cutting the standing timber and investing the proceeds elsewhere than by growing more wood volume on these trees. This is especially true for the mature stands where no net growth is occurring. The optimum period in which to harvest such timber is governed in part by considerations of wise use of investment in processing plants, plus the fact that such stands of timber could not all be liquidated at once even if it seemed profitable to do so—the harvesting task would simply be too great. But on a great many small forests, especially farm forests, the owner has little economic incentive to grow more wood on merchantable trees when the growth rate is so low; and, as a matter of fact, most such owners sell their merchantable trees as soon as volume reaches a point where some buyer is interested. The farmers often do not get the full value of their timber under these conditions, but the slow growth rate discourages more intensive forestry.

Until or unless growth rates of standing trees can be stepped up materially, the incentives to more intensive forestry are weak. A corollary of the foregoing is that increased prices of timber products do not change the situation much if any. When the price of lumber advances, this is an incentive to grow more sawlogs, just as an increase in wheat price is an incentive to grow more wheat. It is also an incentive to cut merchantable trees, thus to cash in the capital accumulated in the tree. More sawtimber can be grown only on standing trees. Since the effect of the increased price of the forest output is offset by the increased incentive to liquidate the standing timber (if merchantable), the incentive for increased intensity of timber management is not much changed.

Forestry may be on the verge of a *biological* revolution. For centuries, Man has harvested the "wild" trees he found growing in forests. His harvesting methods, his use of fire, and other practices have often affected the nature of those forests. But there has been nothing remotely approaching the biological-genetic history and practices of crop agriculture. There, Man has selected plants for centuries, strains of each species have been identified, and good ones have been multiplied. In recent decades, there has been a major development of wholly new varieties—the "miracle" wheats and rices, the hybrid corns and sorghums, and others. In this endeavor, Man has been content not merely to select and multiply, but has created wholly new combinations of desirable qualities in new varieties. There is a continuous struggle against plant diseases and insects, but today throughout the world cultivated plants are pretty much what Man has made them.

Most forest tree species are extremely heterogeneous, genetically speaking. In many species, cross fertilization takes place, and hybrids develop naturally; but even self-pollinated species are usually not pure lines. Some natural selection works out in a stand of young trees, as the more aggressive individuals crowd out the less aggressive ones. But the process is slow, the losers often reproduce, and the next generation is likely to be no better than the previous one. In the last few decades, the field of forest genetics has been growing rapidly. Superior trees have been selected from natural stands, their seed has been saved, planted, and their progeny thereby increased. This is similar to what has been done within agriculture, but the process is much slower for trees than for farm crops because the forest cycle is so long. It takes 40 years or more for almost all species grown in the United States, although some seed may be produced earlier. However, forest genetics is now moving into hybridization on a larger scale, and already has produced some superior varieties, which will be multiplied in the years ahead.

The development of new and vastly more productive strains of trees might greatly change the picture, as far as output in relation to standing volume is concerned. The new tree strains, like new agricultural crop varieties, may prove to be much more productive than the old varieties in favorable environments, but do no better, and sometimes worse, than the old ones in comparatively unfavorable environments. If so, the disparity in growth rates between the most and the least productive sites might well increase considerably.

A great deal of the forest land is owned by the small "other" owners, who seem not to be motivated primarily by a desire for monetary returns from their forests. While it may be assumed that they would welcome a larger cash return, there are serious limits to the time, energy, and capital they are willing to invest in their forests; and intensive forestry for increased output of timber products would have to demonstrate that it did not diminish the recreational or other values of the forest that are the primary motivations of this group of owners.

For a substantial proportion of all forests, regardless of ownership and regardless of production of timber products, outdoor recreation will be a continuing and an increasing usage and demand. Many large forest industry firms have found that it is good public relations to open their forests to recreation use by the public; many have made special investments to facilitate such recreation use. In the public forests, under multiple-use management, outdoor recreation must be given an increasingly important role as one of the forest's outputs. To a substantial extent, good forestry for timber production is also good forestry for recreation, but there will undoubtedly be areas and instances where there will be some conflict, and increasingly outdoor recreation will be the dominant management consideration.

In the past few years, there has been a mounting public concern over forest aesthetics. Many conservation and other groups have been outraged at the appearance of some recently harvested forest sites; they see large volumes of wood left on the ground, the ground torn up and denuded, soil erosion setting in, and the whole looking like a recent battlefield. The forester may point out that the wood left behind is valueless or worse, that a new stand of trees will shortly become established, that the erosion is only temporary, that some trees must be harvested, and that any harvesting will leave some temporary scars. He may argue that the "battlefield" instances are relatively uncommon, and that most forest harvesting is done with more concern for the environment. But some conservationists have been unconvinced. A particular conflict has been aroused over the practice of clear-cutting. In some forest situations, the forester will point out that the kind of forest that develops after selective cutting is not a desirable one; in his view, it is better to cut and remove all the merchantable stock, and then cut the others and plant new seedlings or seeds to develop a different type of forest, one that is more productive of the kinds of output he seeks. These arguments have not been accepted by some conservationists, who not only deplore the interval between the cutting of a stand and its reestablishment but sometimes condemn the kind of forest developed by the planting of a single species.

A somewhat different, but closely related, controversy has developed over forest management in wilderness areas. Since the passage of the Wilderness Act in 1964, several million acres of land have been set aside as permanent wilderness. However, there are other large areas that have wilderness characteristics but are not protected from other uses by a "wilderness" designation. Some groups strongly oppose timber harvest in such areas, arguing (correctly) that the wilderness aspect of the forest would be destroyed by timber harvest.

All of this, and related policy issues and controversies, have made forestry an exciting field of resource management. One may reasonably expect new methods of forestry to evolve, on public and private lands alike, in the next several years. Aesthetics and recreation will almost surely rise on the scale of values, and sawlogs and pulpwood decline, at least relatively.

# CHAPTER EIGHT

# Miscellaneous Land Uses

The "big three" of land use, as far as area is concerned, are grazing, forestry, and cropland with 34, 32, and 23 percent respectively of the area of the 48 contiguous states. These three include 89 percent of the total area, leaving but 11 percent for which some other use is primary. To these three must be added an "important two"—urban and recreation use, which together account for only 4 percent of the total area, but which directly affect far more people than any others.

When these five uses are accounted for—as they were in the foregoing chapters—7 percent of the land area of the 48 contiguous states is left for all "other" uses. The only common denominator of these remaining uses is that each accounts for a relatively small area; however, area is only one measure of importance, and these uses cannot be ignored.

The variety of demands on land and the variety of uses actually made of it are a constant source of wonder, even to one reasonably familiar with land use in the United States. We need not only cemeteries, but pet cemeteries as well; not only recreation areas but rifle ranges. In addition to embracing a large number of highly varied uses, the "other" category includes a sizable amount of land whose use can most reasonably be described as "none." This idle land, of which some extremely limited use might be made, is touched on at the end of the chapter, following a brief discussion of a few of the larger miscellaneous uses.

## WATER STORAGE AND MANAGEMENT AREAS

There has been a great increase in man-made water storage areas in the past generation in the United States, and unless they are over 40 acres in size they are included in the "land" area. Today there are about 2 million farm ponds occupying about 4–6 million acres of land, some of which was previously used for crops, pasture, or woods. These farm ponds have numerous uses: first of all, they provide water for farm animals in seasons when water would otherwise be scarce; they often provide local recreation; they may be used as a source of water for fire fighting; they have wildlife values, and they have modified the life of farm people in many ways, especially in areas where natural water bodies are limited. Almost all of these farm ponds have been built since the early 1930s, and most of them with some form of federal financial assistance.

The number and total area of man-made large reservoirs have also increased greatly in the past 30 years. The Corps of Engineers, the Bureau of Reclamation, the Bonneville Power Administration, the Tennessee Valley Authority, and other federal agencies have each built many large reservoirs. Some reservoirs have been built by the states, and some by cities for a municipal water supply. The estimated total land area has been reduced by more than 5 million acres in the past 30 years, in part as a result of these reservoirs and in part as a result of more accurate measurements and determinations of land area. The total area in large reservoirs is now well over 10 million acres. Some of these reservoirs and some floodways and diked areas are classed as "flood control land," taking up more than 6 million acres of "other" land.

A special situation is being created by the small artificial lakes that are being constructed in many suburbs. Presumably their acreage is included in the urban use category. Such lakes are often strong selling points for the new suburban homes around them. In many cases, however, no provision is made for their permanent management; it is impossible in many instances to find out who really "owns" the lake. In other cases, house buyers within the subdivision are required to join and to help support a citizens' organization that has responsibility for managing the lake.

An artificial body of water, whether small or large, does require management if it is to continue to be usable. Drainage of fertilizer and other materials into such water bodies often stimulates algae growth, leading in some cases to eutrophication, and the lake becomes, literally, a stinking mess. Under some conditions, an artificial body of water can be a great attraction and a real asset; under other conditions, it may be a nuisance. Management to prevent nuisance development is not easy, but clearing up a befouled reservoir is still more difficult.

Another kind of problem arises when artificial water storage is necessary for municipal water supply, and the reservoir often has to be located outside the municipality. The result is often political conflict and bickering; no one loves a reservoir, especially one that is designed to serve someone else and that does not lend itself to multiple-purpose use.

TRANSPORTATION

Streets and alleys often occupy a third or more of the land area in urban use. There are many ways in which the area devoted to such transportation arteries can be reduced without sacrificing transportation service. Considerable savings could be achieved by clustering houses within subdivisions or by reducing subdivision discontiguity. If home, work, shopping, recreation, and other land-using activities were not so widely scattered and disassociated as they now are, less travel would be needed, and urban transportation areas could be smaller.

Highways and roads were reported to occupy somewhat more than 20 million acres in 1964. This area has increased somewhat since then, owing largely to the construction of the interstate and other limited-access roads, which usually have wide rights-of-way and are voracious consumers of land. However, the area in highway rights-of-way has not increased nearly as much over the past decades as has the volume of traffic and the quality of the roads because much of the increase in transportation capacity was achieved by widening, paving, and otherwise improving the actual road surface within the right-of-way. Moreover, although many major highways, especially near large cities, are overcrowded and lack the capacity to service traffic demand promptly, a large proportion of our highways have a substantial excess capacity. Many rural roads could handle several times their present volume of traffic, without requiring improvement and without producing congestion.

Somewhat more than 3 million acres is used for railroad transportation. The greater part of this area is within rights-of-way through rural areas; such rights-of-way are nearly always unused for other purposes, although occasionally a little hay may be cut on them. In a country where land was scarce, some of this land could be farmed, but this is impractical in the United States in most cases. Some of the railroad acreage is within cities or adjacent to them. Large assembly yards, repair shops, storage areas, and other uses occupy valuable land; in recent years, one of the most interesting land use developments has been the sale by the railroads of air rights above their tracks, and the construction of office buildings or other structures thereon.

About 1½ million acres are included in airports; this does not include the relatively large area around many airports where land use is affected by the noise from airplanes. The total area in all airports of the country has not increased much in recent years, but the volume of air traffic (passenger and freight both) has increased greatly. Air transportation, like most forms of ground transportation, has a great capacity to increase output without a corresponding increase in land area. The area actually in airports is only part of the air transportation system; the ground transportation to get passengers and freight to and from the airports also requires a lot of land.

## MINING

Mining is an extremely important, though highly localized, use of land about which we have very little information. Almost no source of data about land use provides information on mining as a land use; the USDA reports from which figure 1 was constructed do not mention it; mining industry data include information on mineral deposits and output but nothing on surface land area involved. Mining includes a great variety of activities; from our viewpoint, they may be classified into those which monopolize the surface of the land and those which are compatible with other surface uses.

Sand and gravel are heavy in relation to value, and, whenever possible, are mined near where they will be used. For this reason, there are sand and gravel workings near all large cities. Dust and traffic may be problems for nearby areas, but the ready availability of low-cost sand and gravel is a real asset to a growing city. Stone quarries, for building stone, are somewhat similar to sand and gravel workings, except that high-quality stone, such as marble, is not found everywhere, and has to be shipped to the cities. In both cases, the worked-out deposits leave pits which can be used for other purposes—for artificial lakes for recreation, or as places to bury solid wastes.

Coal and metals can sometimes be extracted by strip-mining methods; the overburden is removed and piled, and the ore deposit is uncovered for use. In many mines, the volume of overburden exceeds the volume of ore, sometimes substantially; and the weight of metals may be a very small fraction of the weight of the ore. At some copper mines, for instance, $1\frac{1}{2}$ tons of overburden are removed for each ton of ore, and the latter yields only about 16 pounds of copper. The excavated areas become man-made miniature Grand Canyons and the waste piles man-made mountains. Some of the coal strip-mining areas have had their surfaces "restored" to the extent that forest production is possible and some have provided useful recreation lakes and areas. But some areas have not been restored, and from some, especially in mountain areas, the movement of sediments downstream has been large and damaging.

Where coal or metals are extracted by tunnels and shafts, some surface land is required by the mining operation, but the ore extraction takes place under land whose surface may be used for other purposes. In some cases, the underground diggings have collapsed after coal or ore removal was completed, and surface subsidence has occurred, with consequent damage to improvements on the land.

Oil and gas extraction represents a different land use. On land, oil and gas wells can be drilled, and the petroleum extracted, without prohibiting use of most of the surface for other purposes. In some agricultural and grazing areas, oil derricks or oil pumps may be seen in the fields. There is obviously some interference with these surface uses, but not to the point of making them uneconomic. Oil and gas development has taken place offshore in recent years. Techniques have been developed whereby wells can be drilled in water up to 200 feet deep; such drilling is expensive and requires technical competence of a high order. It is also dangerous to the drilling installations and to the adjacent shoreline. In early 1969 there was a major oil leakage from an offshore oil well in the Pacific Ocean near Santa Barbara, California; the beaches were polluted for miles, wildlife was killed, and there was a great public outcry. Other such incidents are highly probable in the future; greater and more precautions, which will be costly, can reduce but not eliminate the risk of such accidents.

A special oil situation has developed within recent years along the north coast of Alaska. Major oil discoveries have been made, and in the summer of 1969 the State of Alaska sold oil leases for over $900 million in cash bonuses, plus continuing royalties which should amount to much more. Additional discoveries and sales are highly probable. This is a unique and difficult area in which to explore for oil; it is tundra, which is a complex and brittle ecosystem, and it is underlain by permanent ice, sometimes to a depth of several hundred feet; and disturbances to the surface often lead to a melting of the ice. Problems will arise not only in getting the oil out of the ground but also in getting it from the well to market. Floating ice increases the risk of damage to ocean tankers and of oil spills, with consequent damage to shorelines; pipelines across permafrost areas pose the risk of severe damage to the areas involved. The Alaska oil situation will pose difficult management and policy issues for many years.

An oil source that has not yet been exploited but that has been on the horizon for decades is the oil shale deposits of Colorado, Utah, and Wyoming. The amount of oil is very great; the problem is that, thus far, methods of extracting it have been too costly. Retorting methods are the most nearly economically practical at present, but these would result in mountains of spent shale, which would almost surely erode and fill streams with great quantities of sediment. Some of the shale land is privately owned, but much is still federally owned; the shale deposits vary greatly in richness, in thickness, and in depth of overburden. Many ideas have been advanced for extracting the oil in situ—by various controlled combustion methods, or by nuclear explosions, and others.

Petroleum is an extremely important resource in the modern world—many would say an indispensable one. Wherever it occurs, there will be interest in its extraction and sale; where deposits are large, as in Alaska, values are great and pressures for development are irresistible; but it often creates serious land and water pollution, and its extraction and transportation will almost surely come under increasing public scrutiny and control in the coming decades.


## DEFENSE

Official reports of the General Services Administration state that over 23 million acres of land within the United States were used for military functions of defense in 1968, and that an additional 7 million acres were used for civil functions of defense. Military bases, which are located in nearly all states, range from relatively small and relatively intensively used sites to very large ones used for developing and testing missiles and other weapons.

From time to time, critics have claimed that the area used for defense purposes is excessive for the need. It has been charged that the military services have public lands reserved for their use or buy additional private lands rather than use lands they already own; it is further charged that the services do not relinquish land when they no longer need it. Such statements were made by President Nixon in early 1970. Given the bureaucratic and procedural methods of the federal government, one would expect land acquisition to be pushed with more vigor and more success than land disposal. The area used for defense purposes may well increase.

IDLE LAND

For most of the land listed as "other" in figure 1, the most accurate brief description of its use is "none." Whatever value such land might have for a particular use is so limited that it would be misleading to classify the land by that use. Most of this idle land is desert, swamp, marsh, bare rocks, or tundra. The areas of this kind of land that are specifically reserved for wildlife and for recreation are classified as such, and what is left in "other" produces little for direct human use, and in most cases little for use by any form of life. Some of this land could conceivably be used some day as sites for homes. Some areas may have mineral possibilities not yet detected; some may be reclaimed or diverted to other uses, but only on a relatively small scale.

Land that is idle but important is usually included with other land uses. Cropland, for example, included more than 50 million acres of idle land in 1964; some of this was high-class cropland, all was usable for crops and had been so used within relatively recent times. An unknown area, but several million acres at least, was idle within and adjacent to urban areas; this land can be developed someday for urban uses.

# CHAPTER NINE

# What of the Future?

Most of this book has been taken up with a description of present land use, with a little history of how it came to be as it is, and with only a few comments about future trends. In this closing chapter, I look more explicitly at what lies ahead—pointing up general trends and raising questions, but not attempting specific forecasts of future land use.

## THE GENERAL SHAPE OF THE FUTURE

Land use will undoubtedly be affected by a number of demographic, economic, and technical trends that are now under way.

The United States will surely have more people in the future than it has today, assuming no catastrophic war. The 1970 Census shows about 205 million people. A few years ago, most population projections for 2000 included at least 300 million people, some considerably more than that. Since 1960, the crude birthrate (the number of births per 1,000 population of all ages and both sexes) has declined by a fourth, and today most forecasters would probably estimate somewhat fewer than 300 million people by 2000. If birthrates continue to decline, the number at the end of the century could be considerably less than 300 million. However, even if by some miracle the birthrate declined tomorrow to a point that would ultimately mean a stationary population (and it would not have to decline so very much further, to reach this level), the relatively large numbers of young people in our population would ensure a continued population increase for at least two or three decades. For our purposes, it does not matter what the exact population figure will be in 2000 or—to put it differently—the exact date at which any reasonable number will be realized. It seems almost certain that there will be more Americans at the end of the next generation than there are now; and their sheer numbers will put increased demand upon land resources.

There is a widespread consensus among economists that real incomes per capita will continue to rise in the future at more or less the rate of the recent past. Between 1970 and 2000 disposable personal income per capita in real (constant price) terms (which is a measure of buying power) is likely to rise by more than half at a pessimistic low to slightly more than double at an optimistic high. In terms of 1970 prices, average family incomes might reach $20,000 by 2000. For our purpose, it is not necessary to estimate precisely how large the increase will be. The very fact that there are more people with more money will mean an increased demand for a wide variety of goods and services, and some of this increased demand will fall on products from the land. The category least affected by higher average incomes will be cropland because the demand for so many agricultural commodities is not sensitive to increases in consumer incomes. The demand for outdoor recreation, in contrast, will almost surely continue to rise greatly; more people with more money to spend spells greater attendance at many public parks.

Increasing affluence has meant—and probably will continue to mean—an increased impact upon the natural environment. Greater output has required higher energy consumption, for instance; and whether the energy came from coal, oil, gas, or some other source, the additional energy has had impacts upon the environment, both in the area of origin and in the area of consumption. One of the major problems of the future is to devise ways of achieving a high economic output for high material standards of living, and at the same time minimizing the impact upon the environment.

The twentieth century may later be looked upon as the period of the knowledge explosion. Free public education was established as a principle during the nineteenth century, but the idea of universal attendance through high school is a twentieth century phenomenon, and the idea of nearly universal college attendance may well be established by the end of the century. Scientific and technological research are now firmly entrenched in every branch of industry. All of these trends will almost surely continue. We may have lost some of our naive faith, or hope, that increased knowledge would solve all our personal or social problems; but we are firmly committed to knowledge as a desirable means of solving problems. A continued growth in knowledge will surely affect land use; the current forecast that increased production per acre of cropland will meet all increased demands for agricultural commodities for at least a generation ahead, for instance, is based on the assumption that agricultural research will continue.

A greater degree of urbanization also seems highly probable, if not certain. The trend has been strongly in that direction for a long time; it is accelerating, not diminishing. There is indeed widespread criticism of the city as a form of human settlement, and the large city in particular; but it is also true that people continue to migrate to such cities. There might be a successful program to modify the present population distribution between very large, large, and medium cities, although even this would be an operation of heroic proportions; but it seems unlikely that there will be a program to reverse the flow of people to cities.

But urbanization is more than a matter of people crowding into relatively compact living patterns; it is also a style of life, or an attitude toward life. In this sense, many American farmers today are urban; college-educated, well-informed, travelled, they are no longer rural in the older sense of the term. Personal consumption habits and personal life styles will almost surely grow more similar to those of people in the larger cities.

All of this points to a society and an economy with greater interdependency among its members in economic, social, and land use terms. Land use within an urban complex today is highly interdependent—what is done on one tract is greatly influenced by what is done on other tracts, and in turn exerts its effects on still other land. This type of interdependence will almost surely grow stronger over the next generation. We may be able to find ways of reducing the negative external effects and increasing the positive ones in a democratic manner. Planned cooperation might produce a more desirable living environment than any individual could achieve on his own. But increased interdependence almost certainly will mean more public controls over private land. The development of zoning over the past generation may have a parallel in the development of stronger and more diversified controls in the future. With more people, larger population concentrations, and a greater social and economic interdependence, it becomes more and more unlikely that each individual will be able to pursue his own ends wholly in his own way. The real issue is to find ways of exerting social control with a minimum of stress and interference on the individual.

A major social attitude of the future is likely to be an increased concern over the quality of the natural environment and a willingness to do something about it, even at a cost. In the past, most people have been more concerned with obtaining the products and services of technology and of the economic machine, and have shown little or no interest in what the production of these goods and services was doing to the natural environment. People wanted big automobiles, fine television sets, a wide variety of household gadgets, enough electricity to run their machines, and a great assortment of other consumption goods; only recently have they begun to worry about what happened to these articles once they were no longer useful, and about what happened to the environment during their production. In the past decade, more particularly in the past five years, there has been a great hue and cry about pollution, waste, ugliness, impairment of the environment, and the like; but it remains to be proved that the electorate as a whole will support effective measures to do something about the problem. Are people really willing to pay higher prices for articles they buy, or higher taxes, or both, to provide a better environment? Surely, some people have not thought it inconsistent to scream for a better environment while continuing personal consumption habits responsible for environmental degradation.

PROBABLE TRENDS IN LAND USE

The most striking aspect of the outlook for land use is its overall stability for a generation or more. A chart showing land use in 2000 will almost surely look very much like figure 1, which shows how land was used in 1964. Net changes from one use to another will be too small to change the general picture. Should some book be published in 2002 with two charts on land use, one for 1964 and the other for 2000, and should the printer reverse them, probably no one would notice. The overall stability will apply to specific tracts of land also—downtown Manhattan will remain urban; most good Iowa cropland will remain in crops; and so on.

The area of land used for some purposes will increase. This will be particularly true for land in urban, recreation, water storage, and some miscellaneous uses. The area used for these purposes may even double by 2000. While this is a relatively large increase for these particular uses, it is still small in the overall land picture. The exact increase in urban area will depend on total population increase, upon the proportion of the increased population that locates in an urban setting, upon the pattern of settlement within the city (especially the lot size and the use of apartments in suburbs), upon the amount of idle land within the generally urbanized areas, upon the rebuilding of decadent older urban areas, and upon other factors. For some purposes it is highly important to estimate exactly how much land will be used by the cities or will be withdrawn by them from other uses; but any reasonable estimate of these factors will not modify the general picture of land use enough to invalidate the foregoing statements about general stability in land use. The total area used for recreation will also be determined by many factors; if the rising demand is met by increased land area, the proportionate increase could be rather large, and yet not change the general picture significantly.

The acreage used for cropland is likely to remain about as now until 2000 or later. Some cropland will be lost to expanding cities, and some of the poorer cropland will pass out of production. But some land will be brought into cropping by additional irrigation or by clearing of trees, and some by new technologies that increase productivity to a profitable level. The net changes will be small; the increased demand for agricultural commodities can be met more economically by increasing output on present cropland. Indeed, the continuing problem will be actual or potential crop surpluses. Even the gross changes will not be large in proportion to present cropland area.

There will be some net losses in grazing and forestry land areas because it is only in rare cases that either of these uses can compete effectively for land that is in demand for urban, recreation, or cropping use. Grazing is nearly always low man on the totem pole of land uses and gets its large area largely by default. Forestry, on the whole, produces a larger annual economic output per acre than grazing does, but has about the same competitive strength. Some of the increased urban area over the next generation will come out of land now classified as used for forestry. But an area that represents a large percentage increase for urban land use will be a very small loss for forestry; moreover, most of the forest land so converted will be land that is not very productive now. The inroads of recreation upon forestry and grazing may be more serious, and will more frequently arouse opposition from the industries losing land, but a doubling of recreation areas would still take a relatively small percentage of forestry and grazing land.

## SOME PARADOXES IN THE COMPETITION FOR LAND

Overall stability in land use seems probable for the future; yet, paradoxically, change in land use is likely to produce more controversy and general turmoil in the future than in the past. The very forces that bring stability also bring a degree of rigidity. The general picture that emerges from this book is one of enough land to readily meet the demands on it for at least a generation—no attempt is made to look further ahead. But this generally comfortable picture may be somewhat misleading; there are already some problems, and they may grow more serious. Merely to say that a person's general health is good does not prove that he has no need of medical or dental attention.

Some of the land use problems were noted in earlier chapters: a lot of land withdrawn by cities from other uses, yet idle and unproductive; a lot of decadent older urban areas; not enough recreation land in total, overcrowding of some recreation areas, serious deficiencies in the supply of parks in the lower-income parts of cities; some crop, grazing, and forestry land eroding or otherwise deteriorating, and some without adequate stands of grass or trees. One should not minimize these problems; they demand and justify more attention and greater investment than they have received. But the United States is still generously supplied with land; we can no longer use it so lavishly and with so little thought for the future, as we once did.

Changes in land use will come with increasing difficulty in the future. The area used for highways may be less than one percent of the total land area, yet for each acre converted from residential to public highway use, the conversion is 100 percent. Even where the conversion is from one private owner to another (rather than from a private to a public owner, as above), the repercussions of the land use change may be considerable. In this day of interdependencies in land use, it is not uncommon for many persons to have an interest in a tract of land that they neither own nor actively use. For instance, let there be a proposal that some of the land surrounding an old house be re-zoned to permit construction of an apartment house; scores or hundreds of citizens, concerned with the effect of the proposed construction on the general character of their neighborhood, or on street traffic, or on crowding in their already full schools, or other aspects of community life, will turn out to oppose the rezoning action if a public hearing is held. Or let there be a proposal to use a swamp or marsh as a landfill area for disposal of solid wastes; again, there will be scores or hundreds of citizens who do not own the land and may never have set foot on it who will feel that they have an interest in the land use and will oppose the change. The electric power companies have found it increasingly difficult to locate power stations and power lines; too large a sector of the public has an interest in every possible location for such plants to be located without objection.

The stability and the interdependencies in land use will in-crease the difficulty of land use changes. Calculations of relative economic values may have some influence, but in many cases the people who will be disadvantaged by a land use change will be unmoved by an economic calculation showing that the national or community welfare will be increased by the change; they lose, and they oppose. The losses may be hard to evaluate. For instance, what harm does the public or a segment of it suffer if an old house with historic and architectural charm is torn down and replaced by a filling station or a shopping center? Some people may feel that they are worse off because they have lost something that enriched their lives; others may consider that the change has left them better off.

Our mechanisms for resolving this type of conflict are not very good. We are likely to see increasing public controls over private land use; the externality relationship will increase in importance and will demand more concern for the general public not directly involved in an existing land use or in a proposed change in land use. The private market will still remain important, although increasingly conditioned by public controls and public incentives. The political process (using this term in a very broad sense) will determine or at least strongly influence many land use decisions. One of the major tasks for social engineering for the next generation is to find ways of bringing all interests to bear on land use decisions and to reconcile opposing and mutually exclusive interests in a better way than we do today.

Another interesting aspect of the present land use situation, and one related to the stability of land use, is the rising competition for land, as measured by land prices. The total value of farm real estate has doubled since 1954; the price of good recreation land has risen at least as much; and the price of land in and around growing suburbs has risen still faster. Governmental action has, directly and indirectly, greatly stimulated these increases in land value. An indirect influence has been the widespread conviction that governmental policy will never permit a repetition of the 1930s or of earlier great depressions. This has led to a confidence in future prosperity and in future worth of property that has affected land values, although it is difficult to express its importance in quantitative terms. More direct governmental actions have been the agricultural programs under which farm owners received substantial payments because they owned land, income tax provisions treating capital gains more tenderly than ordinary income and permitting real estate taxes and interest paid on mortgages to be deducted from income, and guarantees to savers and to lenders, which increased the flow of capital into real estate. Once land values begin to rise, the process is self-fueling; as long as prices rise, ownership of land is remunerative, irrespective of current income. In a great many situations in the United States today, land prices have been bid up to a point where the net income from the use of the land represents a very low return on the value of the land. If the land were sold and the money invested elsewhere, the interest on the investment would exceed the net income that is received from the use of the land. However, a decline in land values is unlikely as long as general prosperity continues.

# A Selected List of Books on Land

BOLLENS, JOHN C., and SCHMANDT, HENRY J. *The Metropolis.* New York: Harper and Row, 1965.

CLAWSON, MARION. *Policy Directions for U.S. Agriculture.* Baltimore: The Johns Hopkins Press, 1968.

———. *The Bureau of Land Management.* New York: Praeger, 1971.

———; HELD, R. BURNELL; and STODDARD, CHARLES H. *Land for the Future.* Baltimore: The Johns Hopkins Press, 1960.

———, and KNETSCH, JACK L. *Economics of Outdoor Recreation.* Baltimore: The Johns Hopkins Press, 1966.

COCHRANE, WILLARD W. *The City Man's Guide to the Farm Problem.* Minneapolis: University of Minnesota Press, 1958.

DANA, SAMUEL T. *Forest and Range Policy: Its Development in the United States.* New York: McGraw-Hill Book Company, 1956.

HALL, EDWARD T. *The Hidden Dimension.* New York: Doubleday and Company, 1966.

HALPRIN, LAWRENCE. *Cities.* New York: Reinhold, 1963.

HIGBEE, EDWARD. *Farms and Farmers in an Urban Age.* New York: Twentieth Century Fund, 1963.

MEYERSON, MARTIN; TERRETT, BARBARA; and WHEATON, WILLIAM L. K. *Housing, People and Cities.* New York: McGraw-Hill Book Company, 1962.

PUBLIC LAND LAW REVIEW COMMISSION. *One Third of the Nation's Land. A Report to the President and to the Congress.* Washington: Government Printing Office, 1970.

RASMUSSEN, WAYNE D. *Readings in the History of American Agriculture.* Urbana: University of Illinois Press, 1960.

SAMPSON, A. W. *Range Management—Principles and Practices.* New York: John Wiley and Sons, 1952.

STODDARD, CHARLES H. *The Small Private Forest in the United States.* Washington: Resources for the Future, 1961.

TAYLOR, LEE, AND JONES, ARTHUR R., JR. *Rural Life and Urbanized Society.* New York: Oxford University Press, 1964.

TUNNARD, CHRISTOPHER, AND PUSHKAREV, BORIS. *Man-Made America: Chaos or Control?* New Haven: Yale University Press, 1963.

U.S. FOREST SERVICE. *Timber Resources for America's Future.* Forest Resource Report No. 14, U.S. Department of Agriculture. Washington: Government Printing Office, 1958.

———. *Timber Trends in the United States.* Forest Resource Report No. 17, U.S. Department of Agriculture. Washington: Government Printing Office, 1964.

WINGO, LOWDON, ed. *Cities and Space.* Baltimore: The Johns Hopkins Press, 1963.

# Index